THE ART OF JON CHRISTOPHER

INTO THE MYSTIC

DRAWINGS AND PAINTINGS FROM 2008-2016

A TRAVELING SHOES PRESS BOOK

THE ART OF JON CHRISTOPHER

INTO THE MYSTIC

DRAWINGS AND PAINTINGS FROM 2008-2016

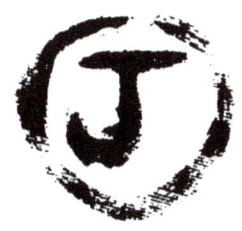

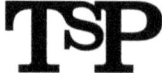

TRAVELING SHOES PRESS
PO BOX 332
Pioneertown, CA 92268

Into The Mystic: The Art of Jon Christopher |
Drawings and Paintings from 2008-2016
ISBN# 978-1-7329205-8-3

© 2021 Jon Christopher
All rights reserved. This book or any portion thereof
may not be reproduced or used in any manner whatsoever
without the express written permission of the publisher
except for the use of brief quotations in a book review.

First Edition | 2021
Book design by Jon Christopher

Dedicated to the mystics, seekers
and lovers of art...

INTRODUCTION

There was a time when I religiously followed the belief system I grew up indoctrinated in… I think most people do that. But there comes a point when you have to leave the comfort of blindly following the family religion and discover what you really believe.

That point came for me in 2008 when I was just into my forties. I grew up as a charismatic evangelical Christian. That included actively believing in being baptized in the Holy Spirit, speaking in tongues, laying on of hands for healing and many other beliefs based on the idea that God is still active today and miracles are a regular part of life…

God. That's a big one. I have personally experienced miracles that had no explanation other than the intervention of some divine entity. But I began to question the constructs that I had learned concerning God. I got into consciousness, and the "mysteries of being" in 2008 after reading a Carl Jung book a friend gave me.

And as I started to peel back the layers of reality that had been constructed by my Christian life I got into astrology, mysticism, alternate realities, tarot, and a number of other interesting avenues of esoteric investigation. I questioned everything.

These pieces of art are souvenirs of that adventure. I created each piece as a meditation on the idea of mysticism. Mysticism, for me, is the belief that there is more to the world than meets the eye. Maybe it's the cosmic dance of the planets altering our consciousness. Maybe it's the World Tree, the flower of life and the movement of the microcosm creating our reality. Maybe it's the tarot sending us messages like some quantum computer. Maybe it's an ineffable idea of something beyond the daily humdrum...

My goal was to spend 2008 to 2015 investigating these mysteries... I thought I'd have it all figured out by then. Well, I didn't get it all figured out, and the mysteries still blow my mind on a regular basis.

I hope you find these drawings and painting inspiring, revealing, and mystifying. Yes, there are plenty of symbolic meanings embedded in many of these pieces that can be decoded and meditated upon. Seek and you will find!

Until later, best of health.

Jon Christopher
The Hi-Desert of Southern California, 2021

SELECTED DRAWINGS

2008

RENEWING THE WORLD TREE

2008

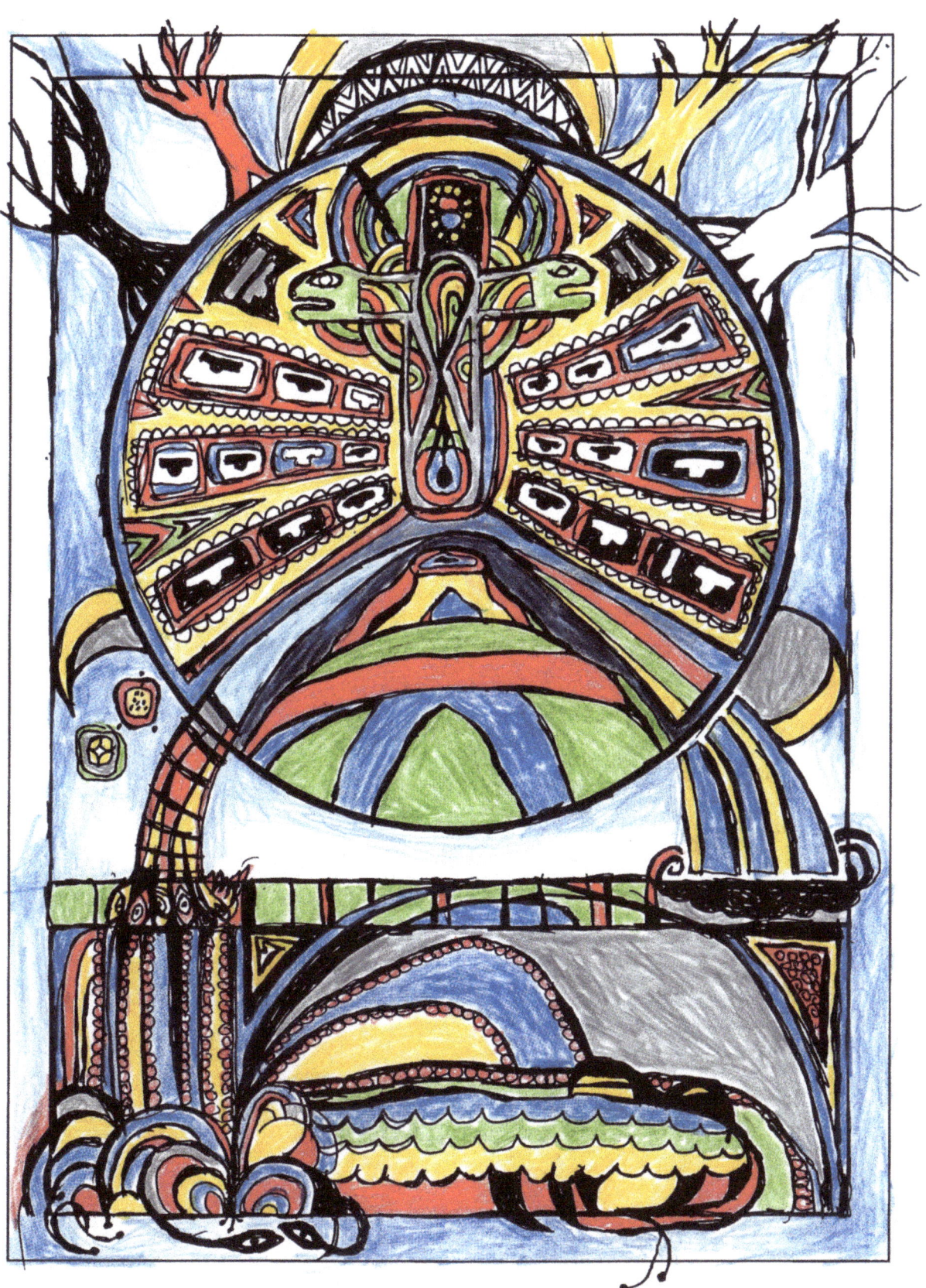

OPHIUCHUS

2008

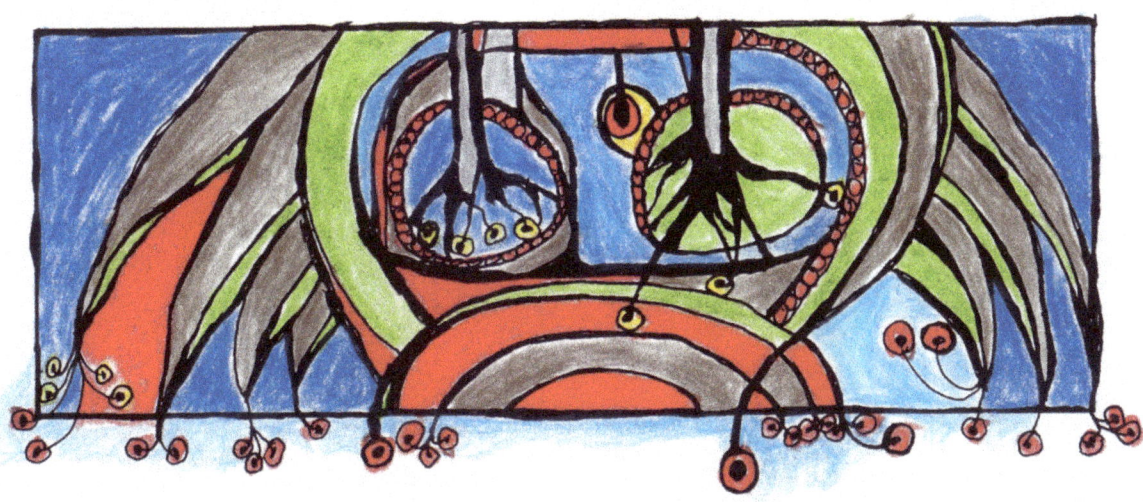

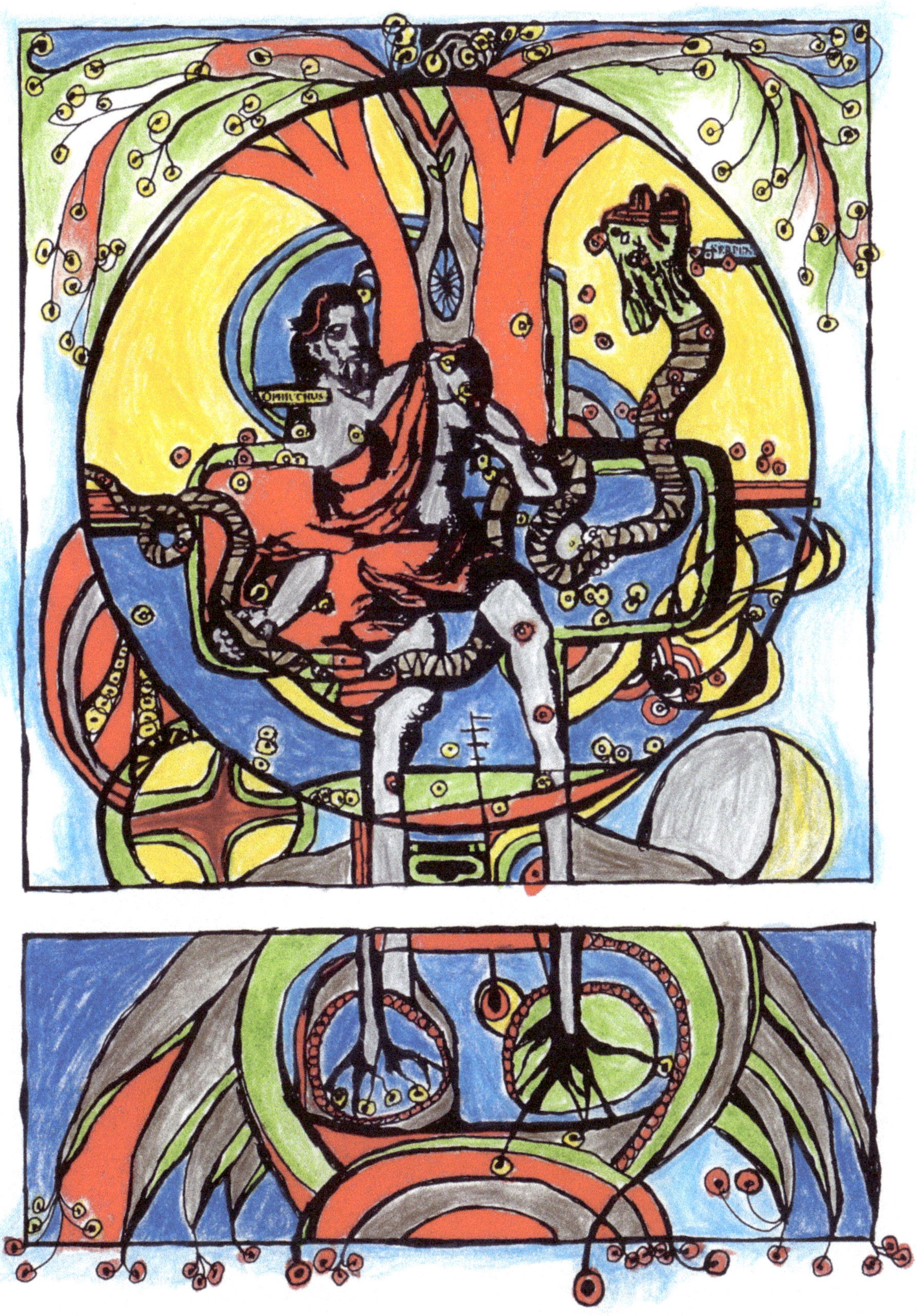

HELTER SKELTER

2008

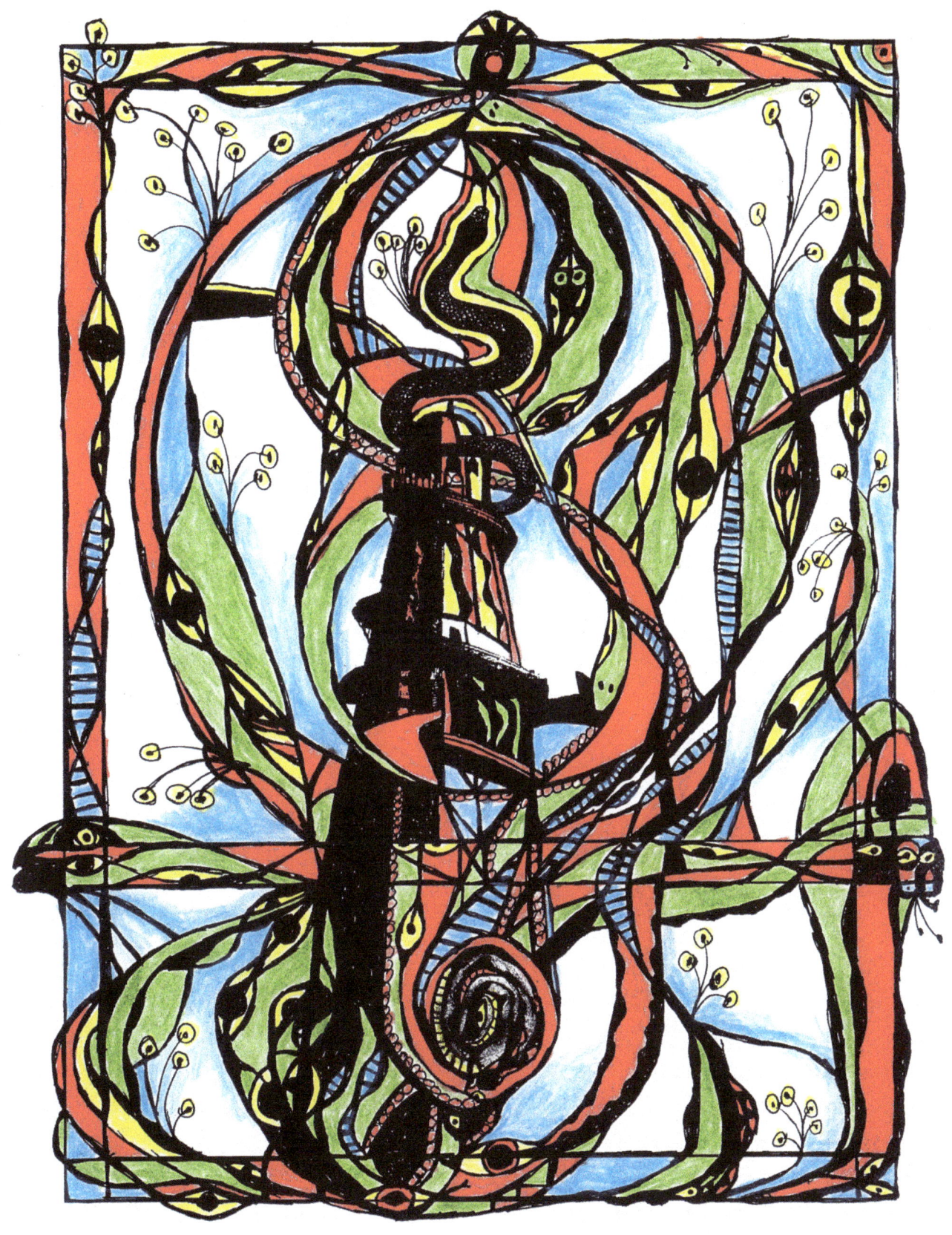

JACOB AND ESAU (THE TWINS)

2008

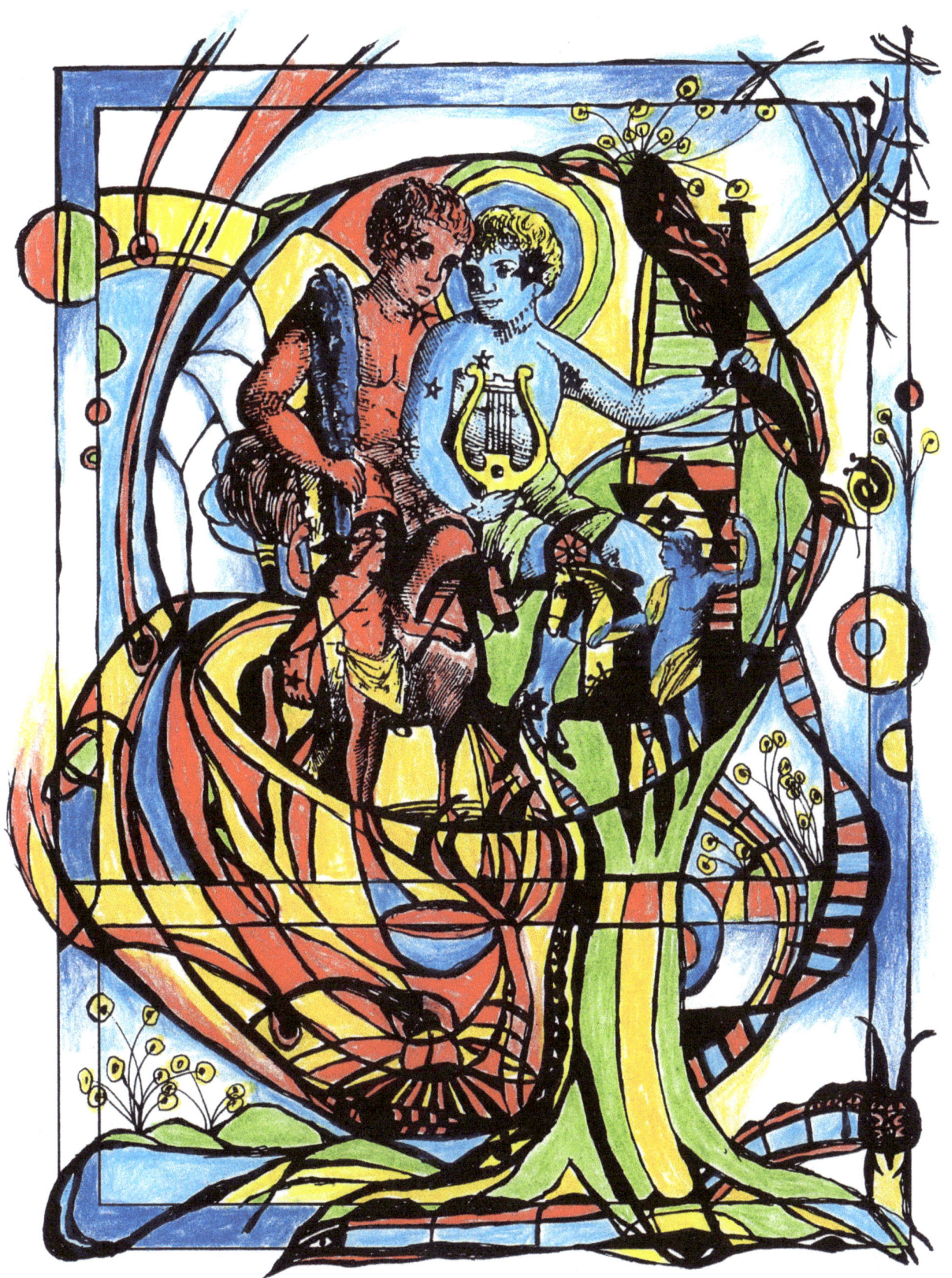

INTO THE MAZE

2008

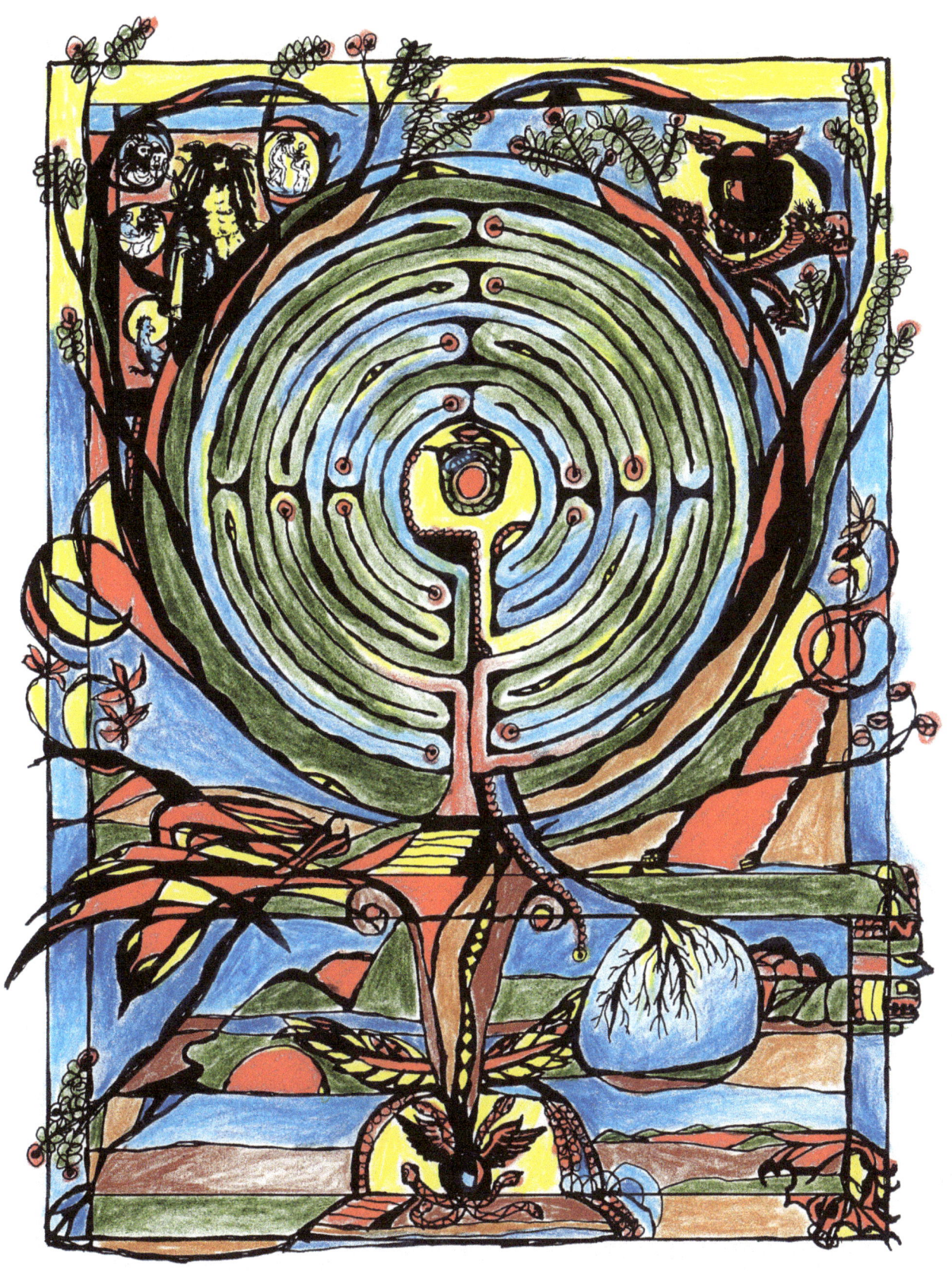

DEATH VALLEY DRAWING

2008

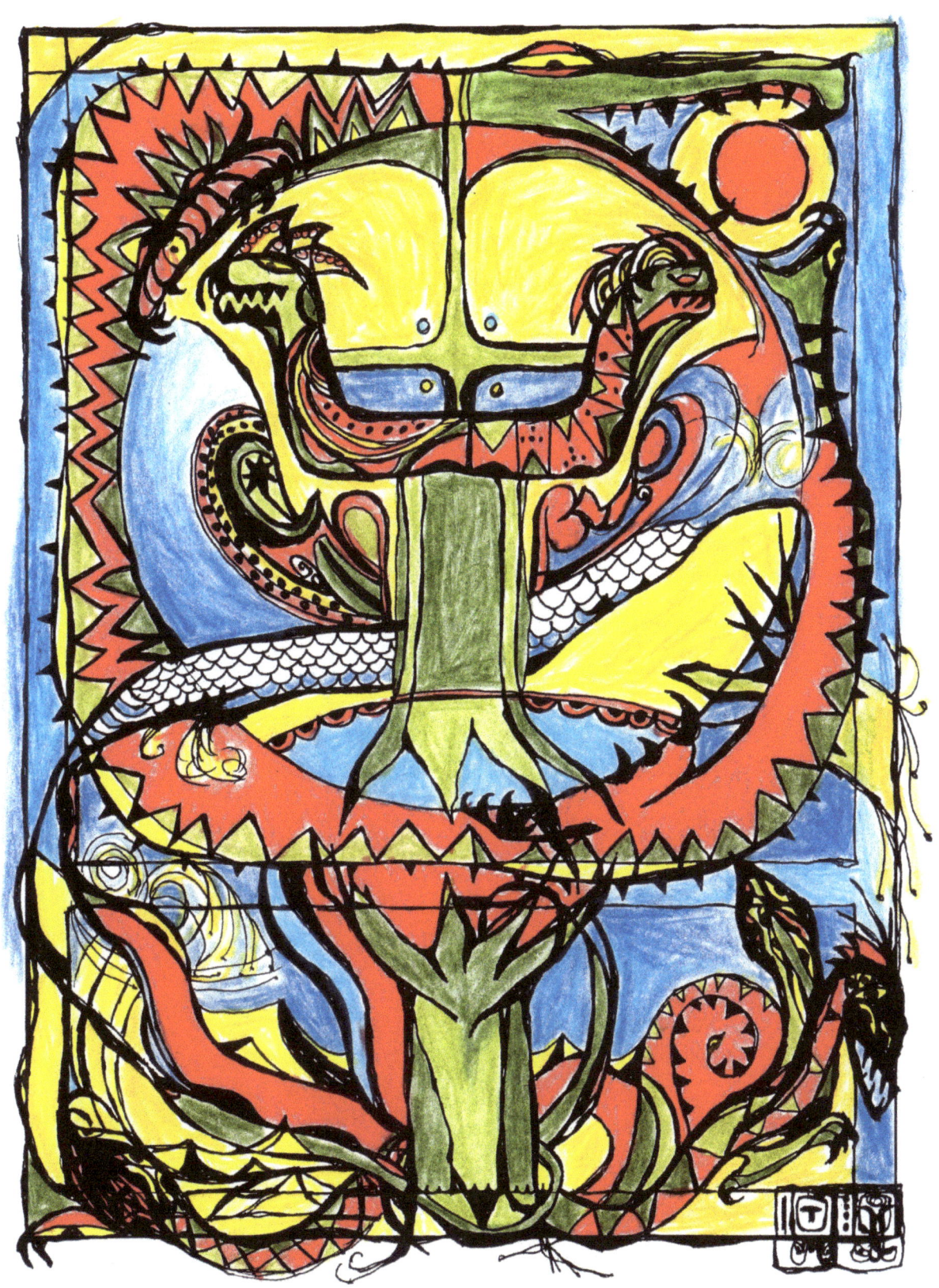

THE DUNES

2008

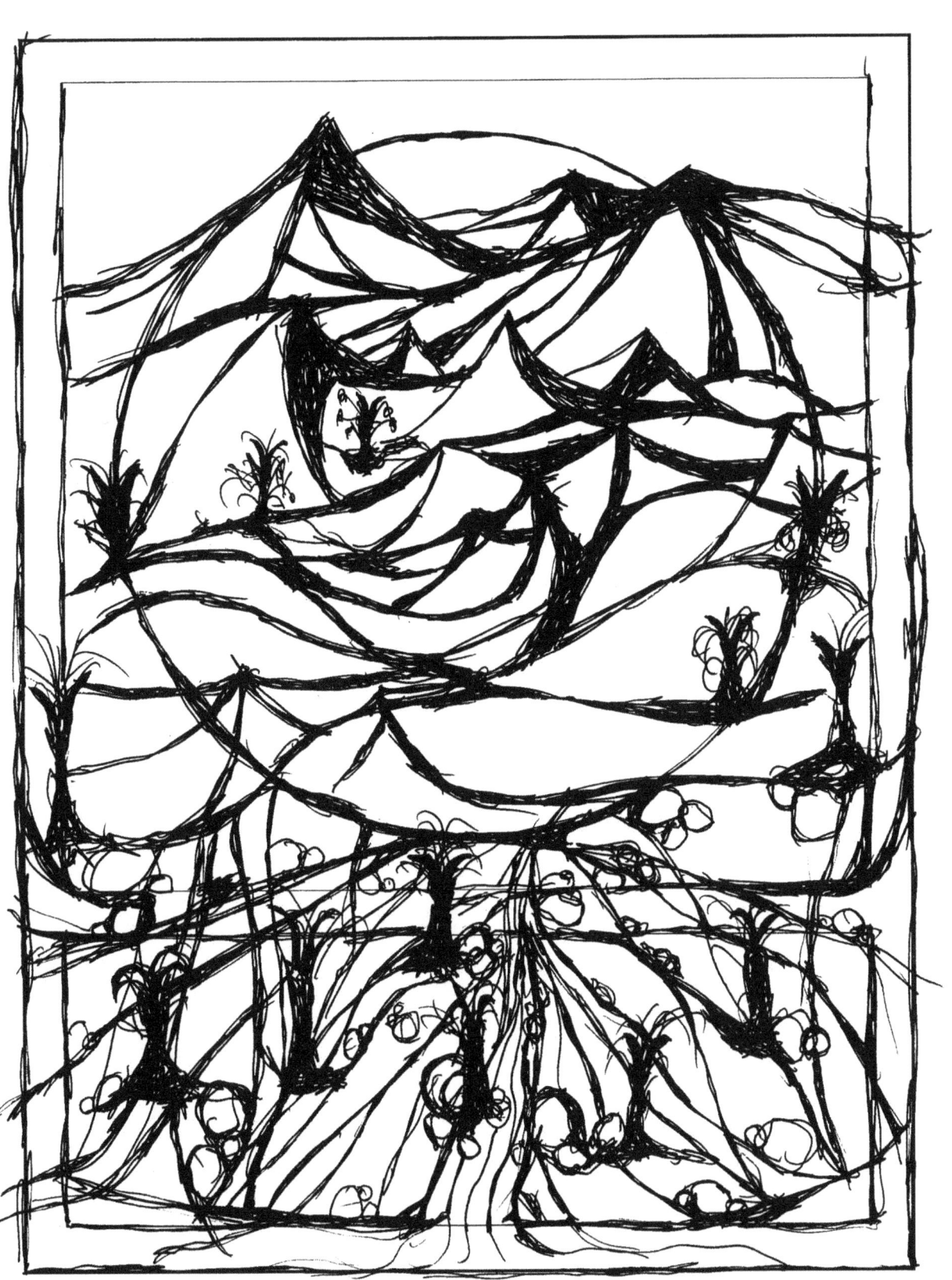

FADING VISIONS

2008

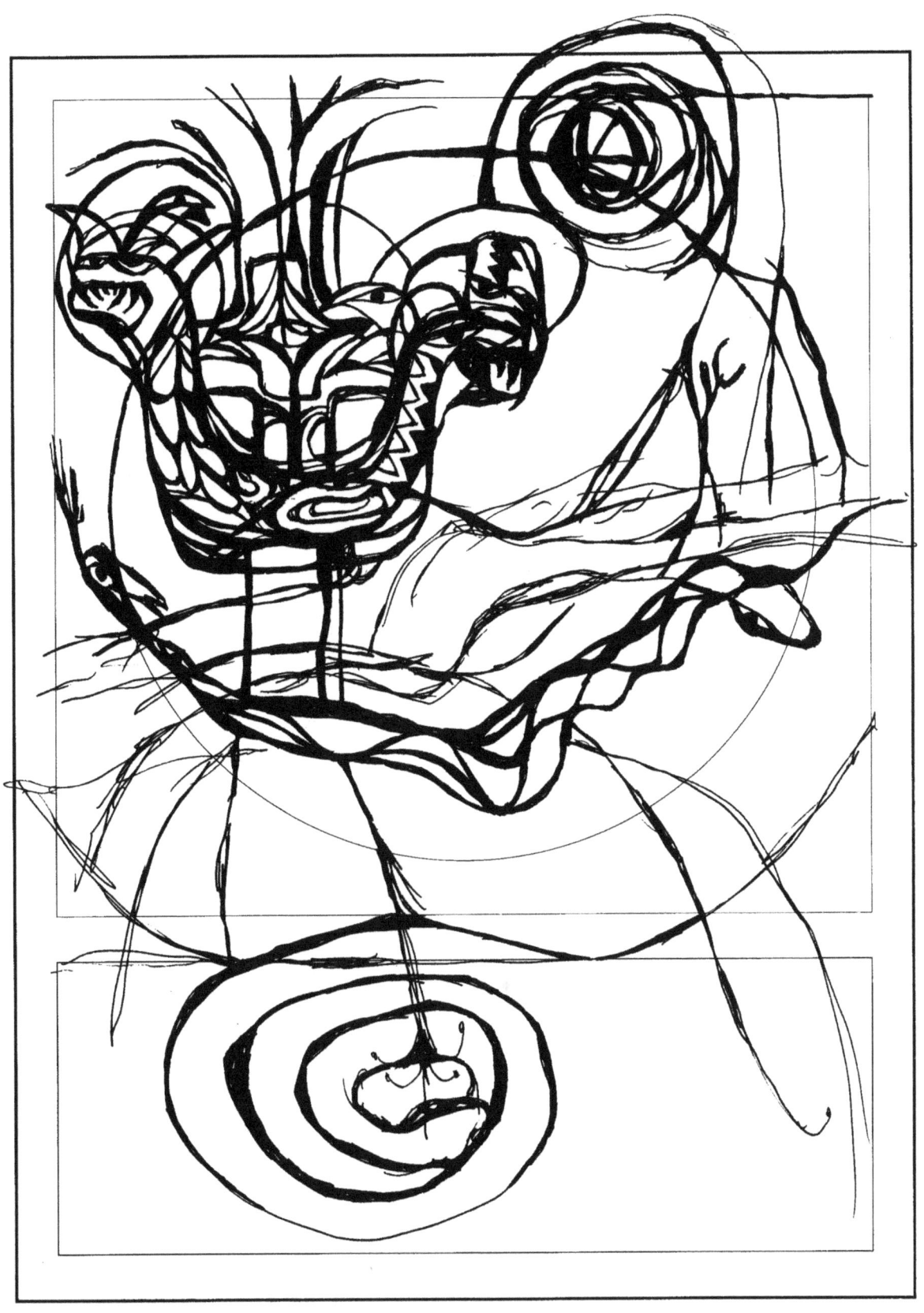

SELECTED DRAWINGS

2014-2016

OUROBOROS AND THE FLOWER OF LIFE

2014

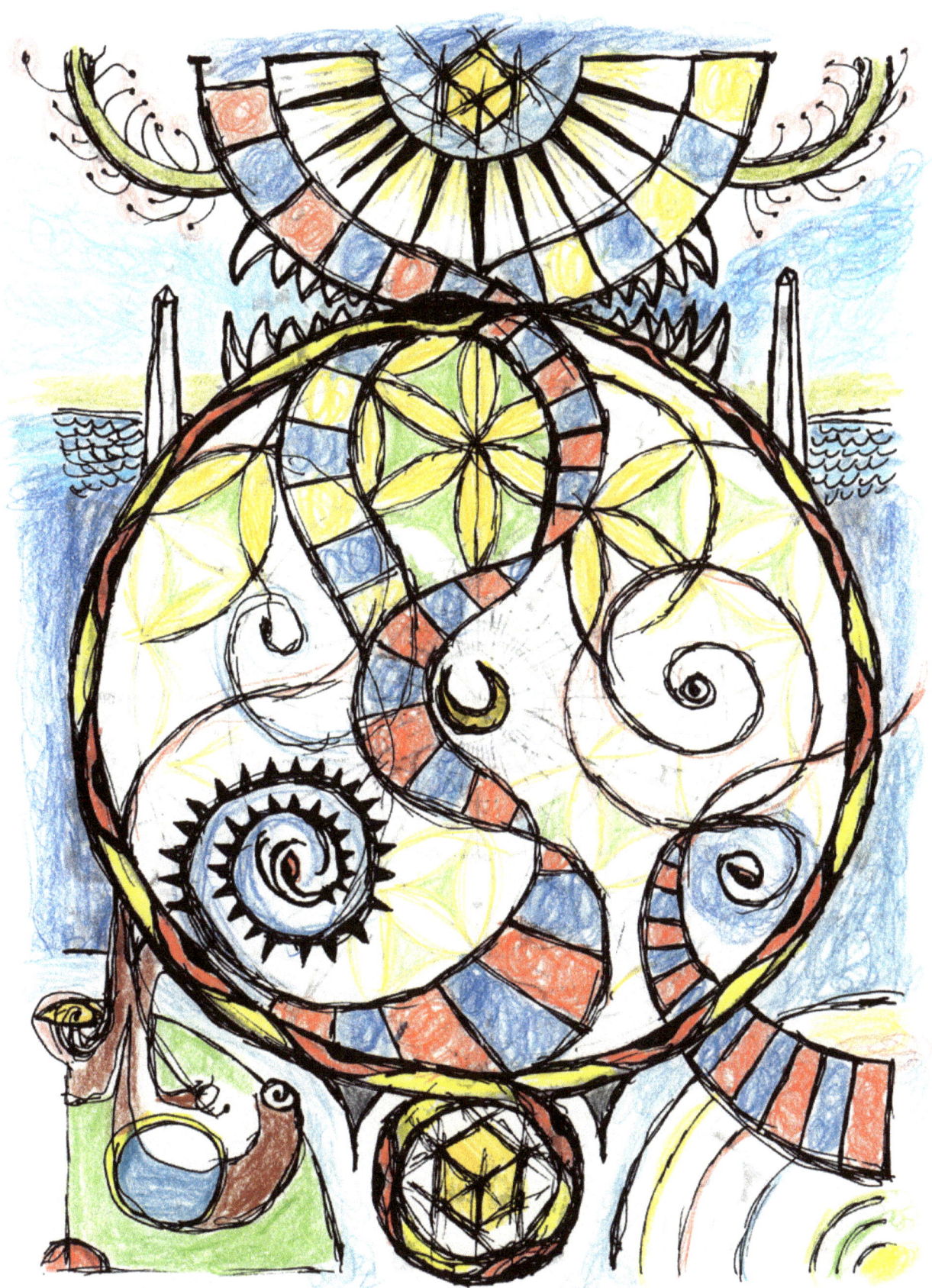

WHEN THE WORLD TREE BLOSSOMS

2014

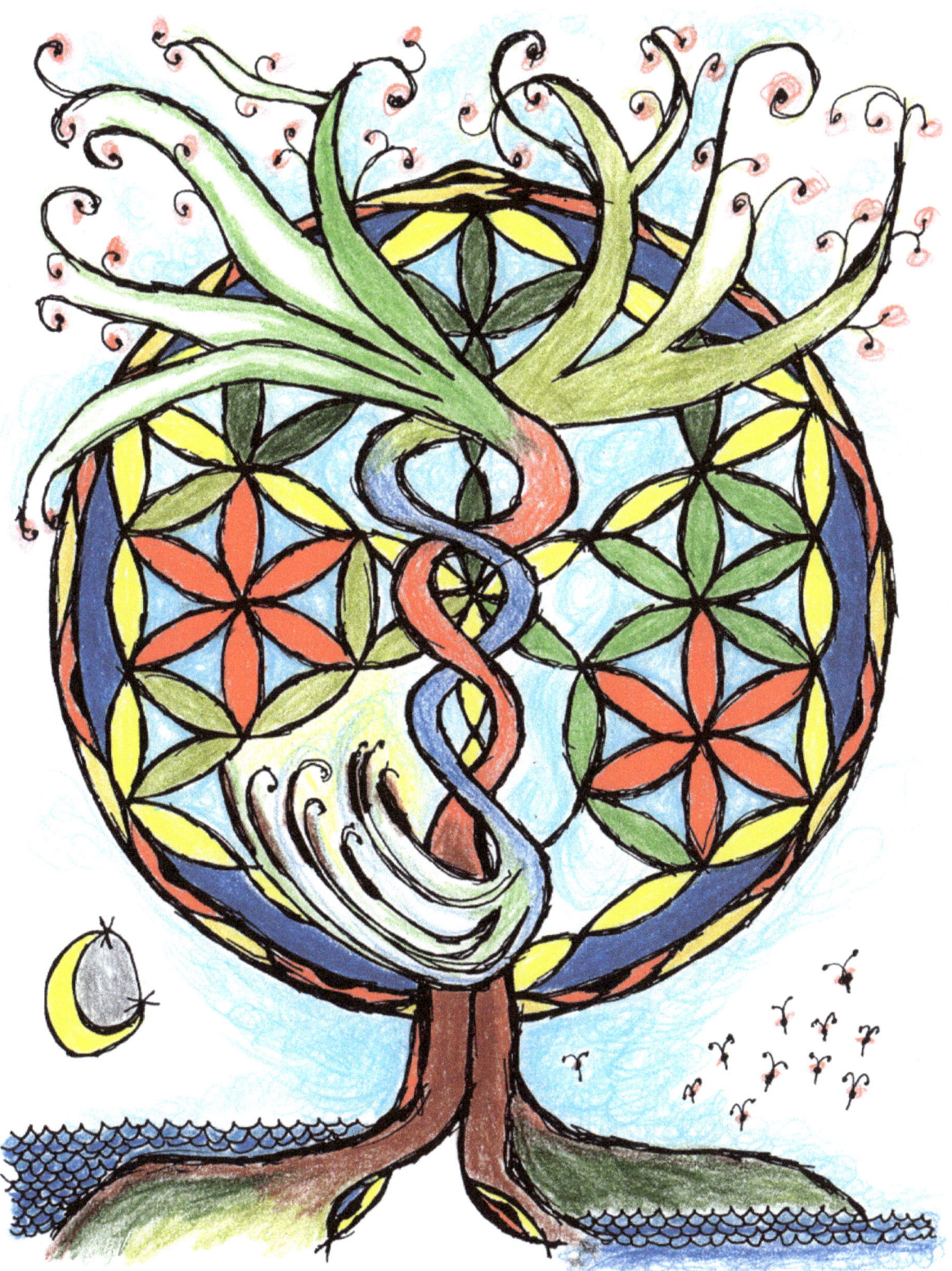

THE DOG DAYS

2014

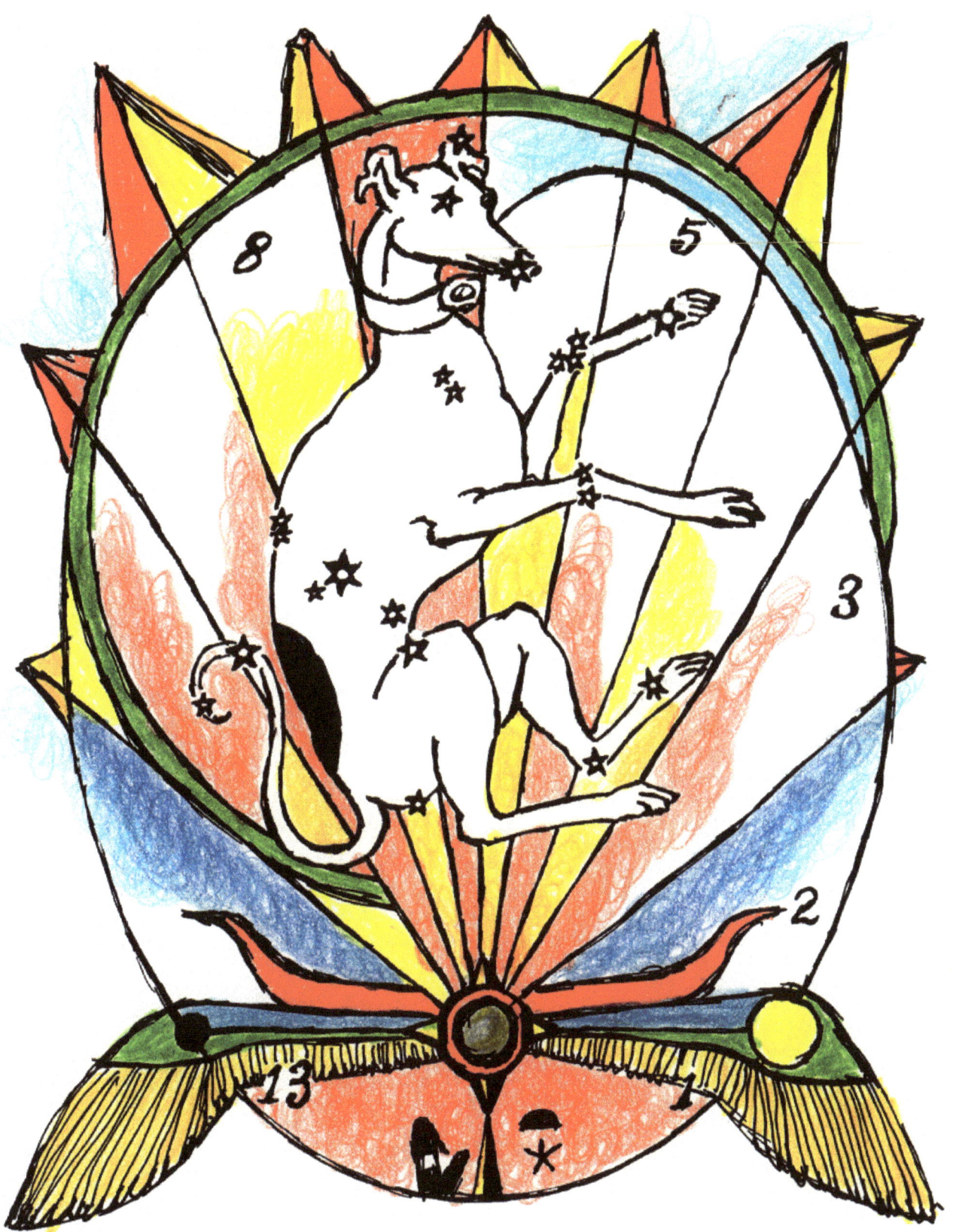

TWO OF SWORDS

2014

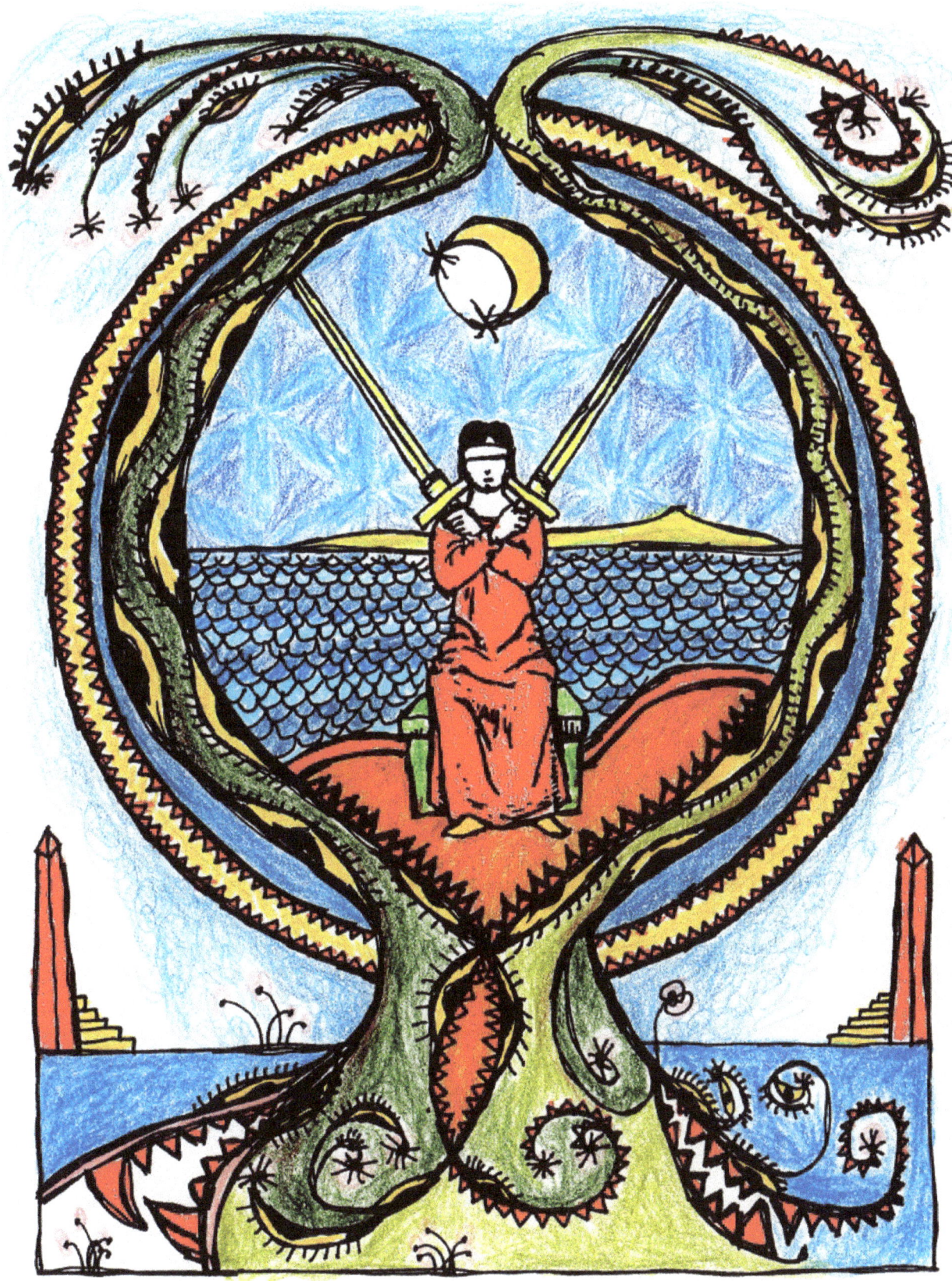

THE TWO OF PENTACLES

2014

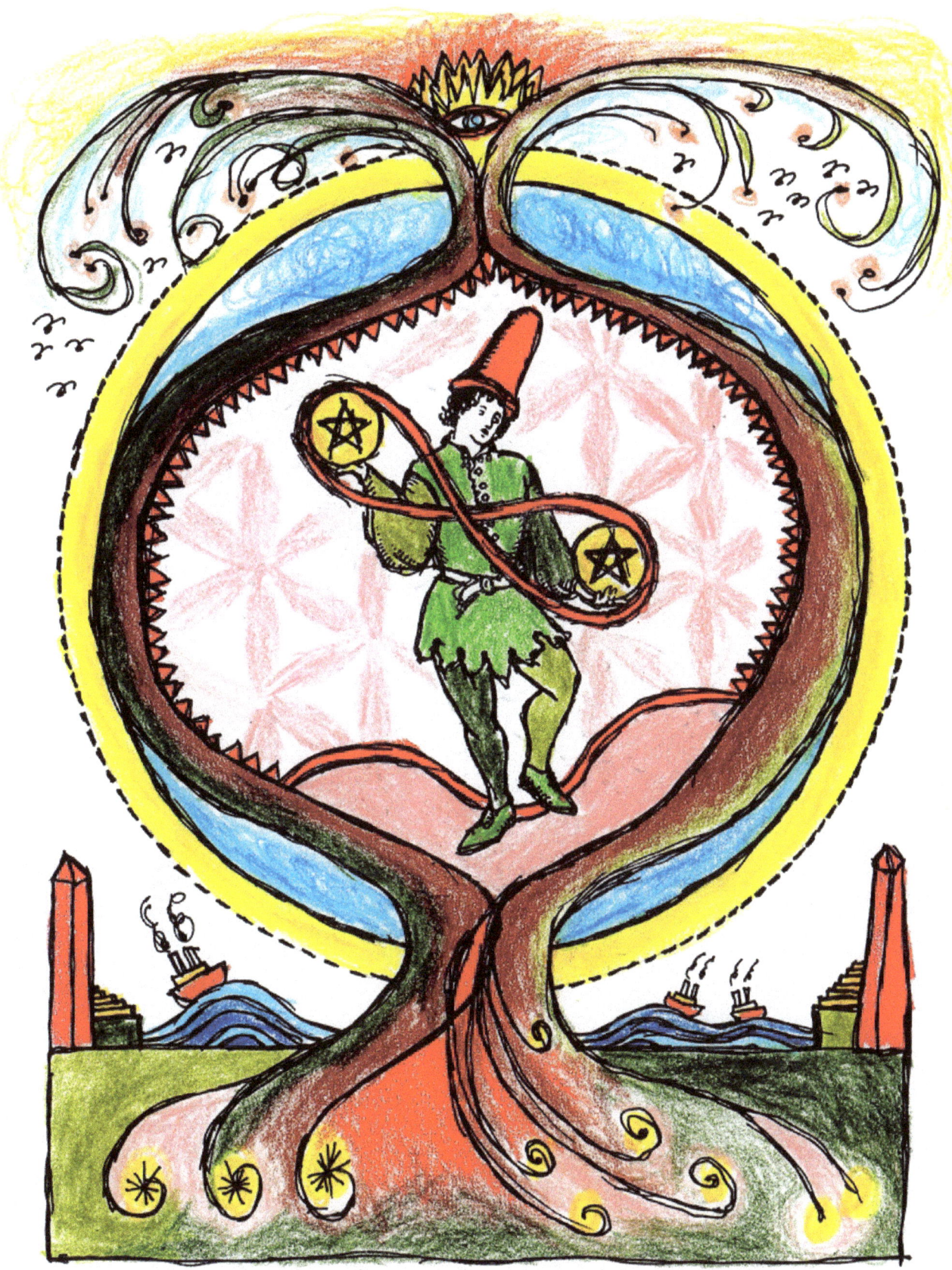

THE HANGED MAN

2014

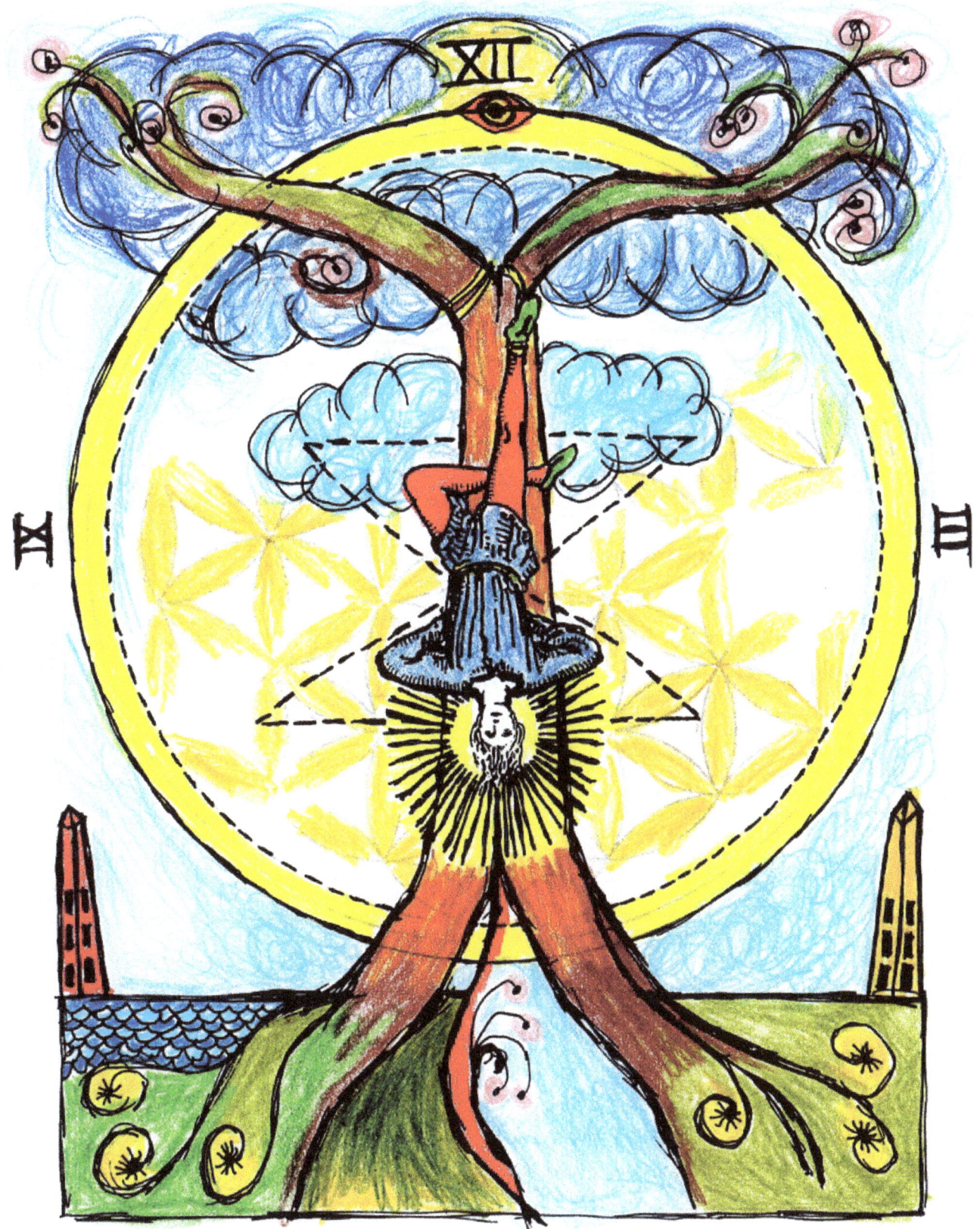

THE WORLD

2014

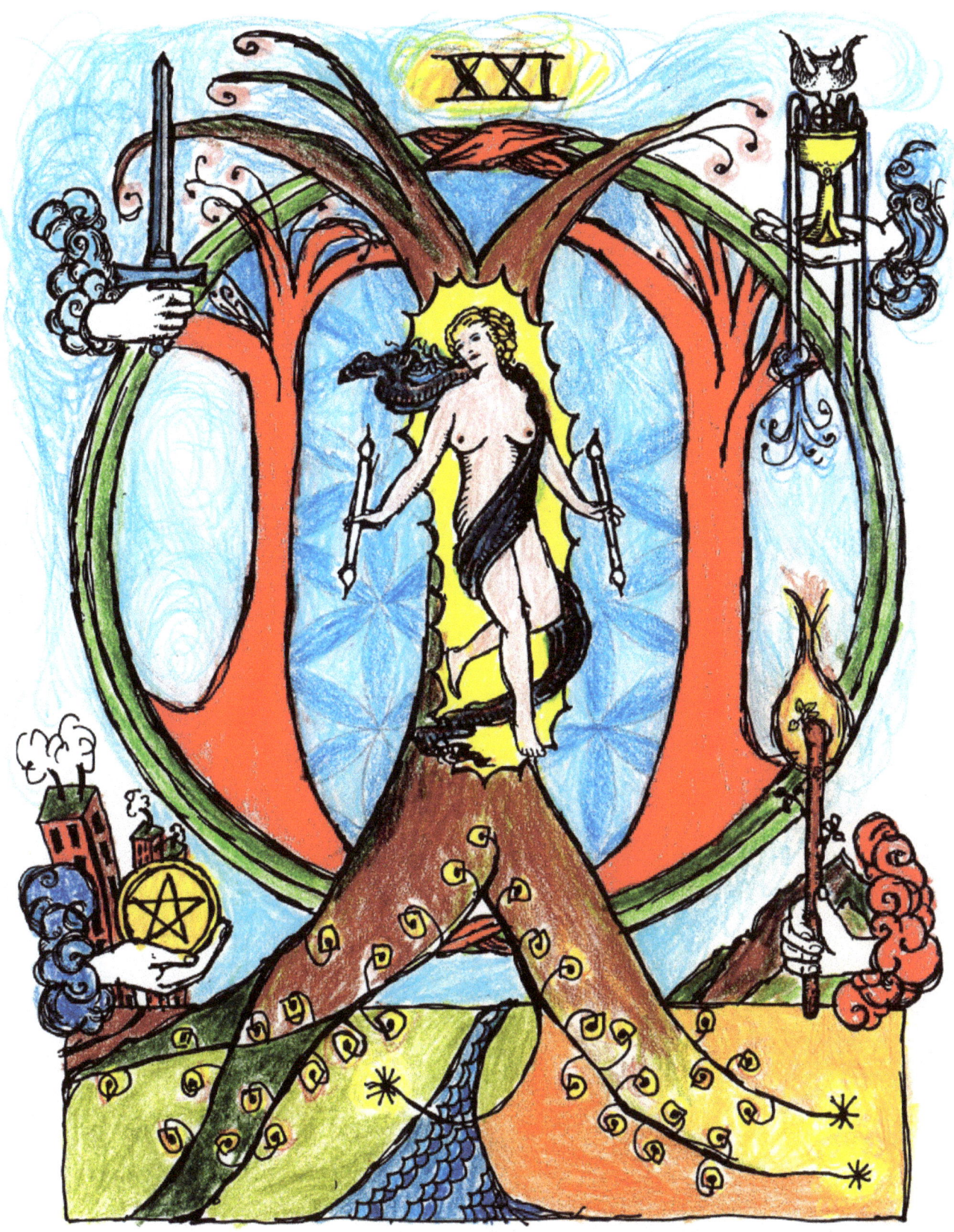

THE GLASS ONION

2015

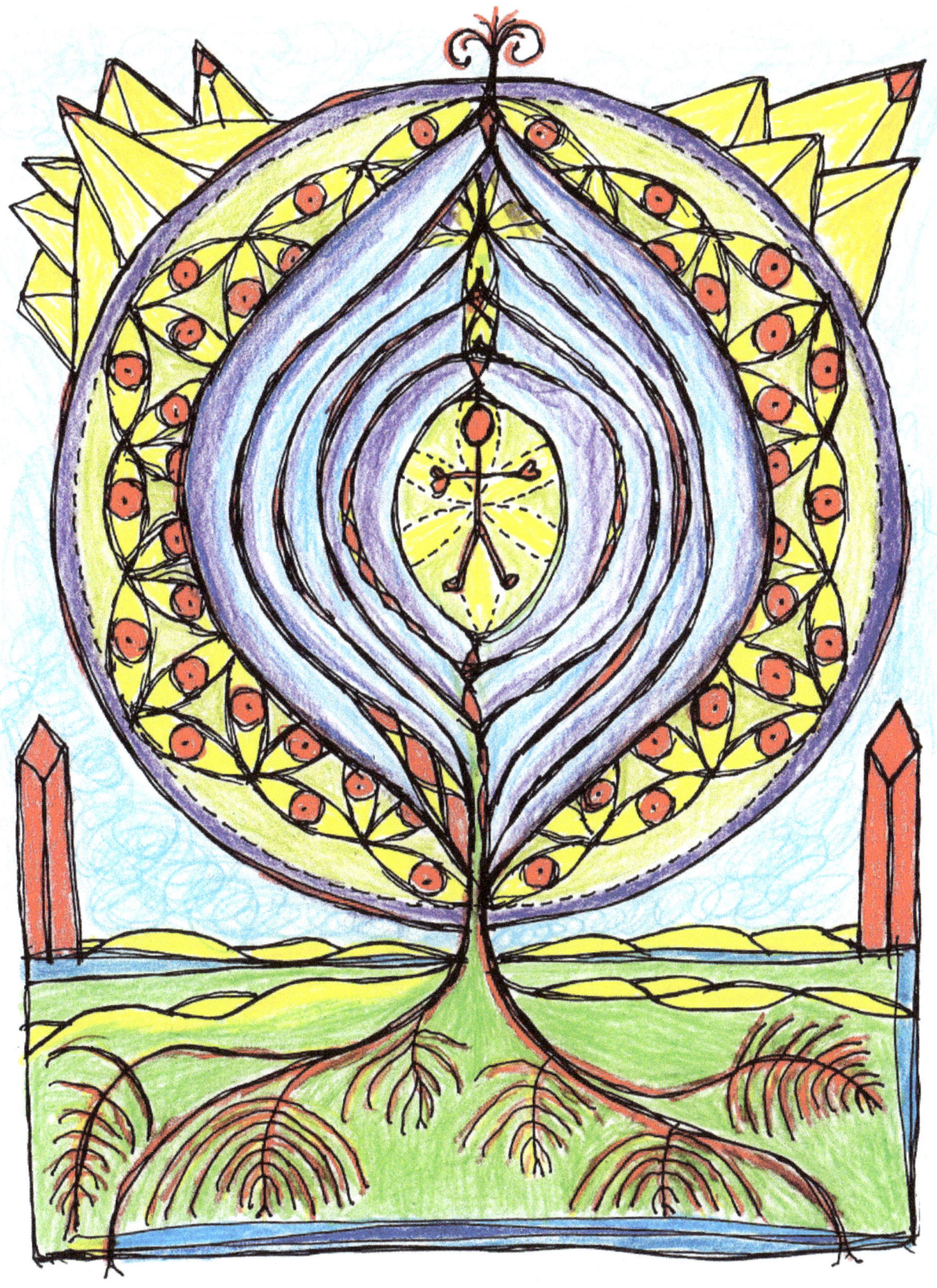

NUMBER 13

2015

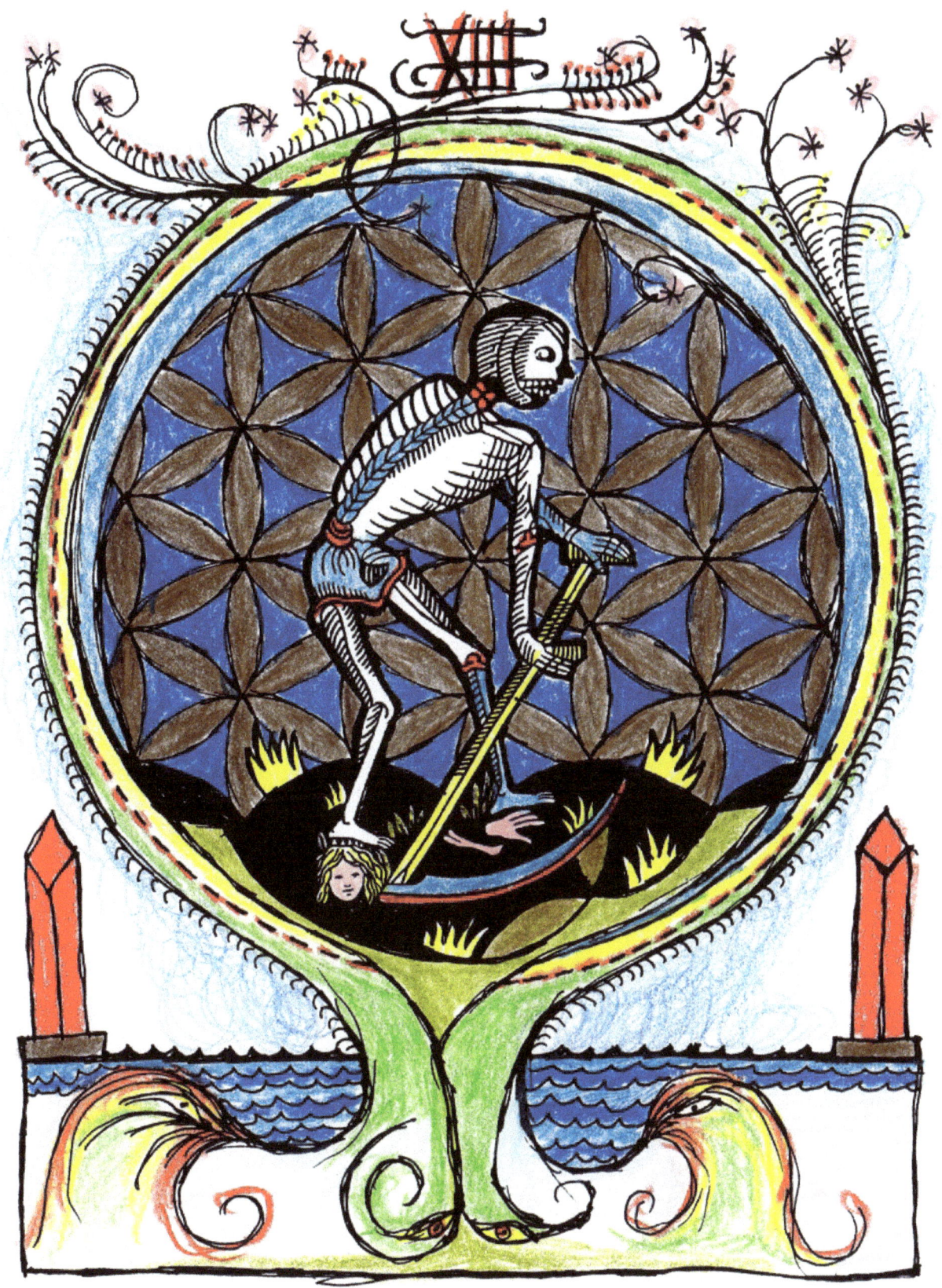

SWEPT INTO THE TWILIGHT

2015

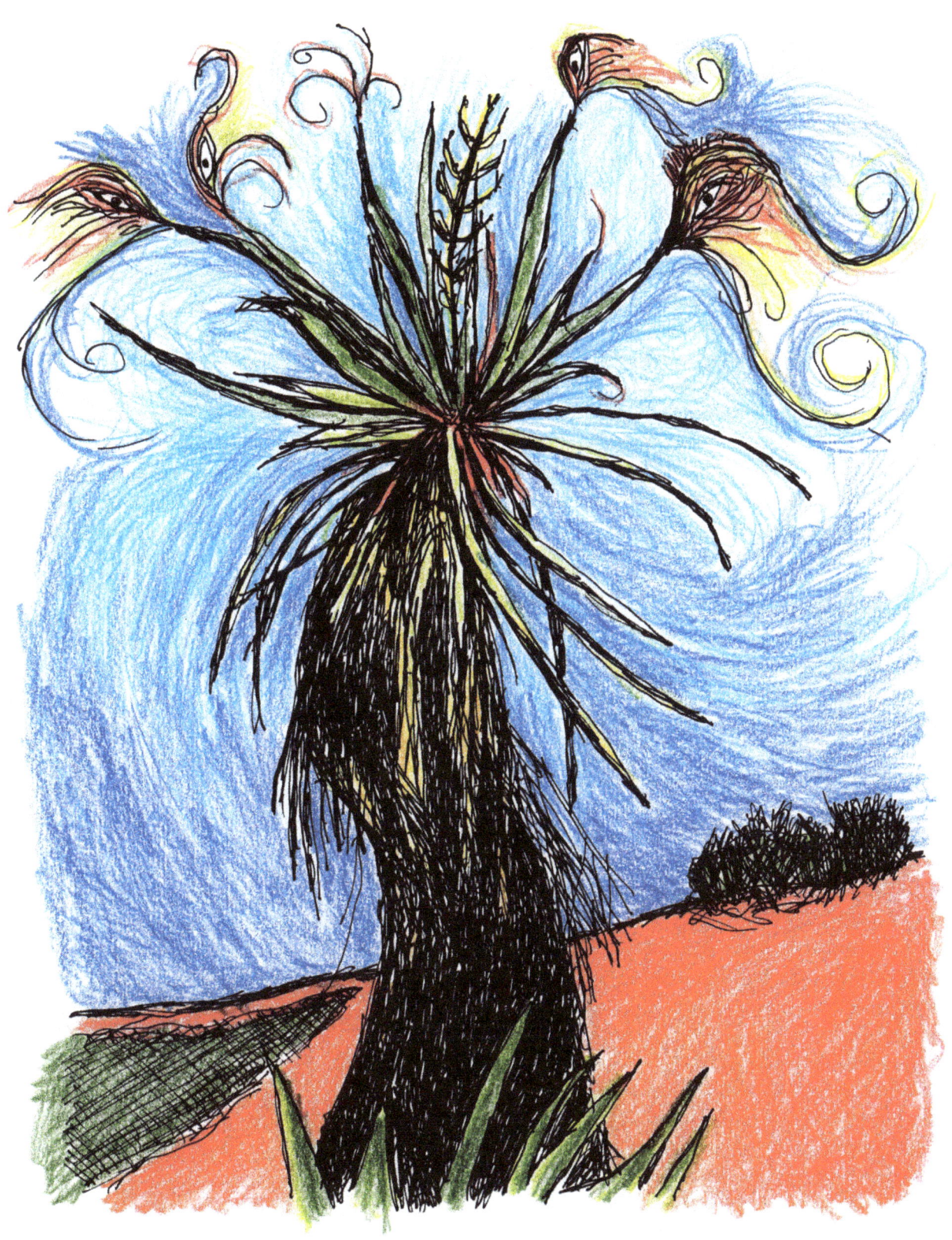

THE JOURNEY INTO THE SECOND SUNRISE

2016

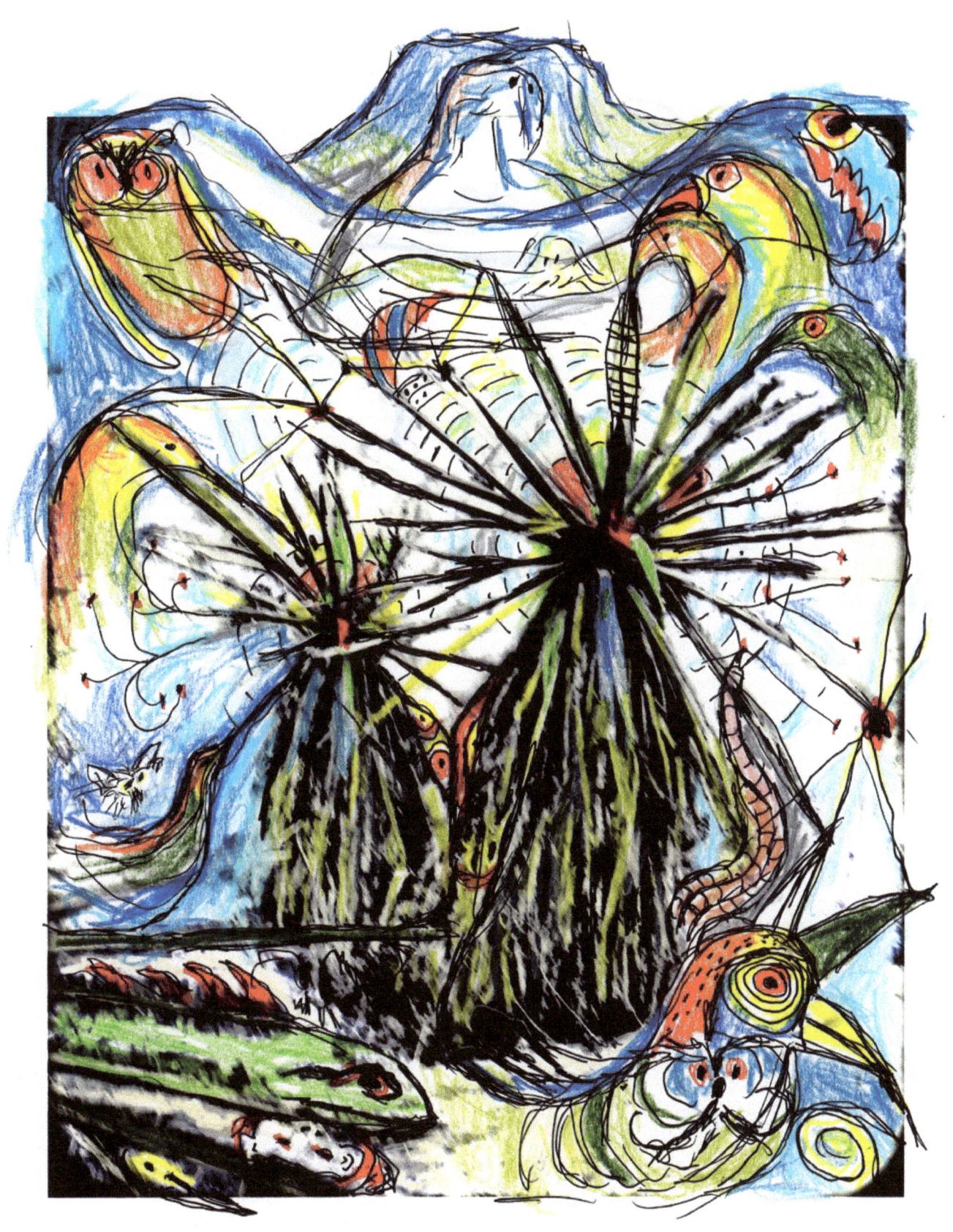

JOURNEY TO VISIT THE WIND

2016

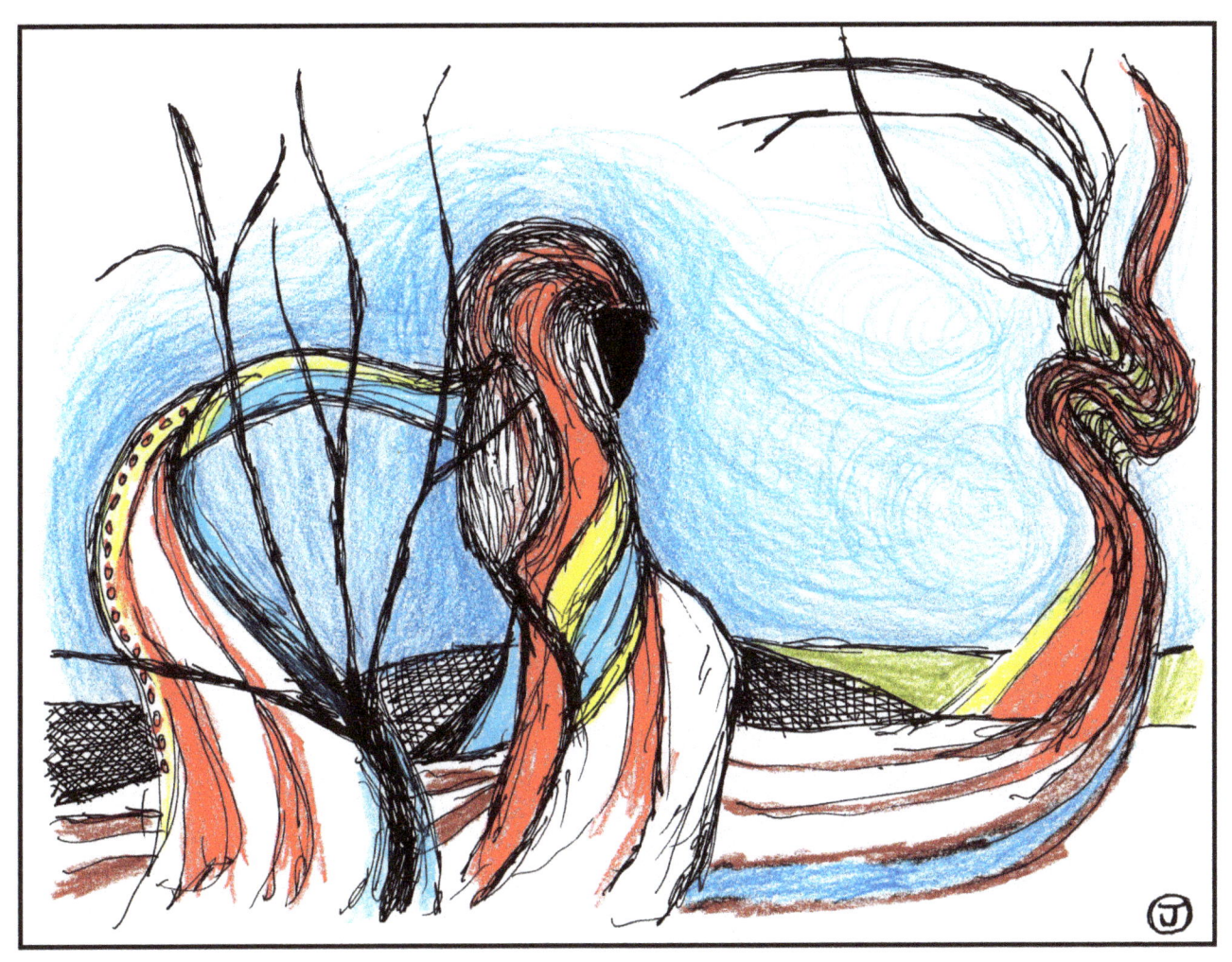

THE YUCCA SHAMEN

2016

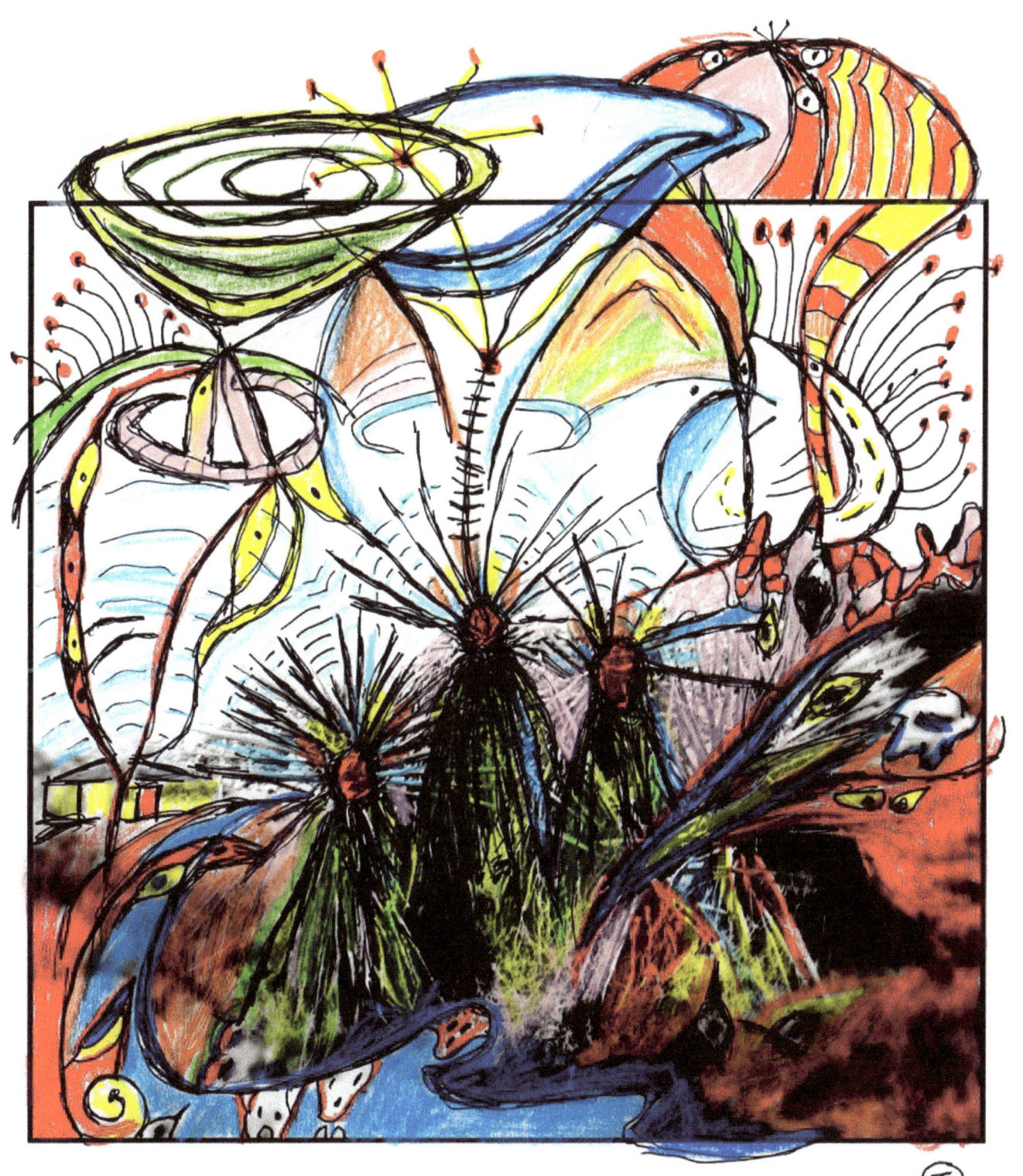

SELECTED PAINTINGS

2015-2016

THE KNIGHT OF CUPS

2015

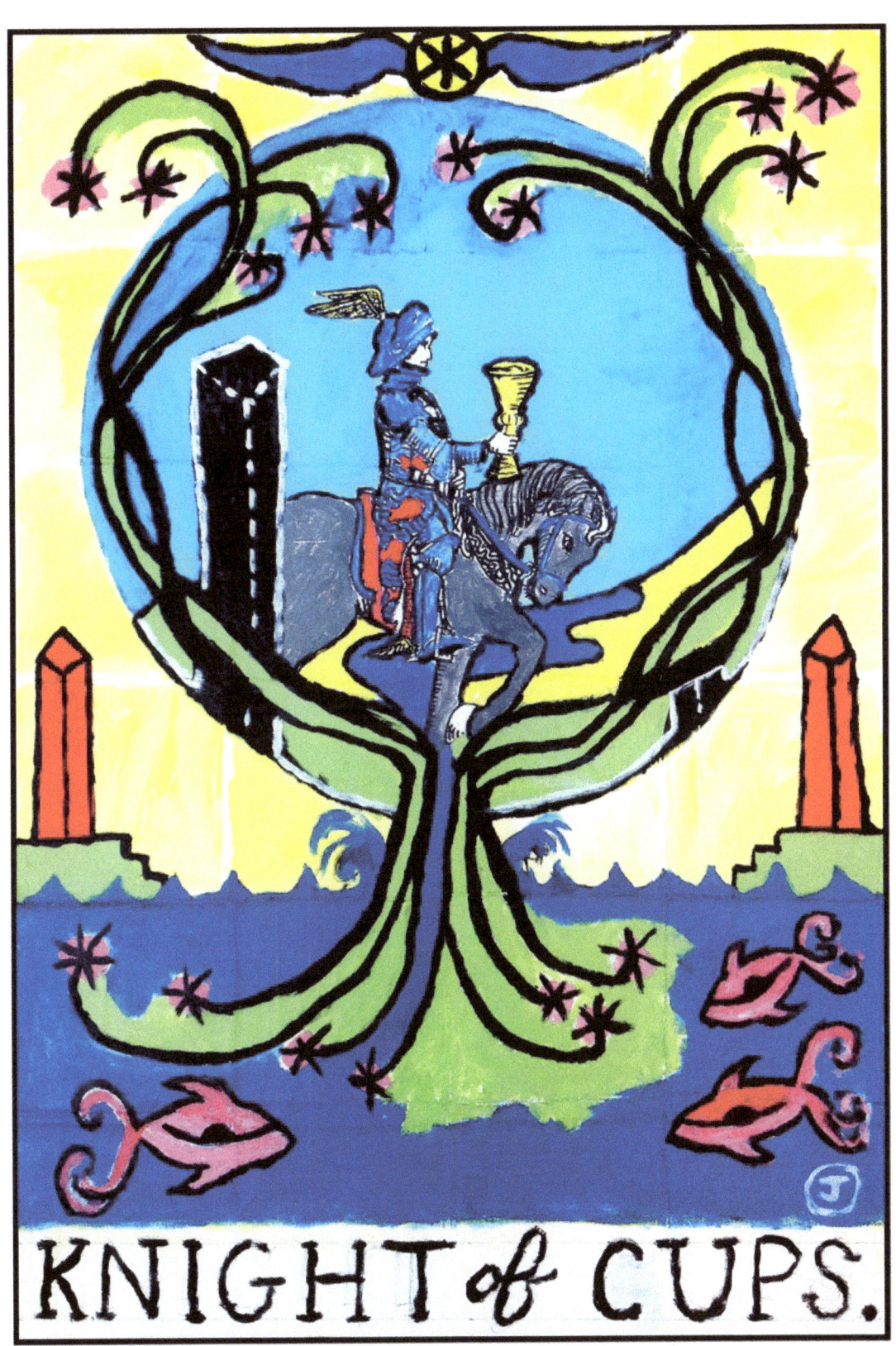

THE TWO OF WANDS

2015

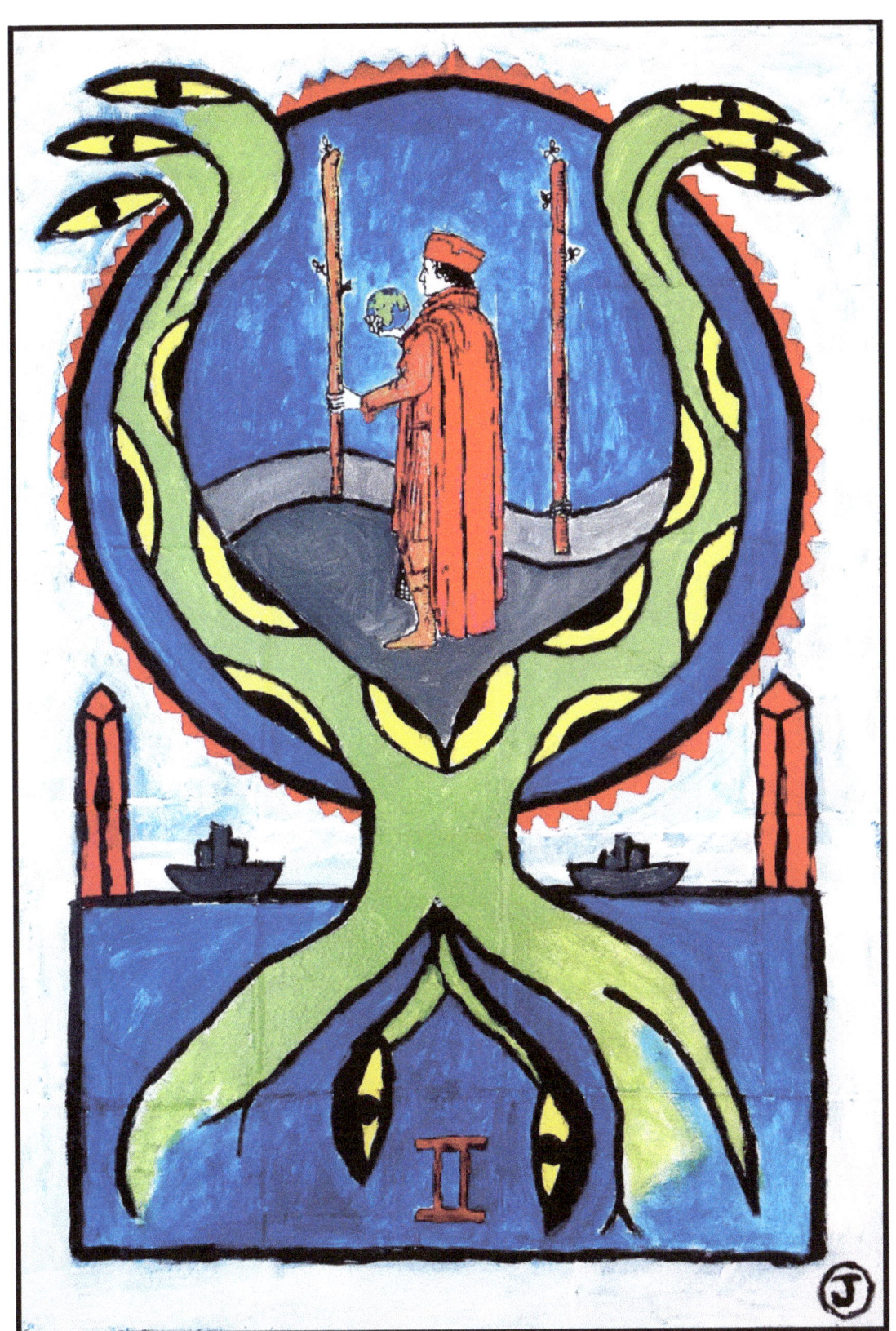

THE FOOL

2015

In the collection of Stephen Joel Jensen

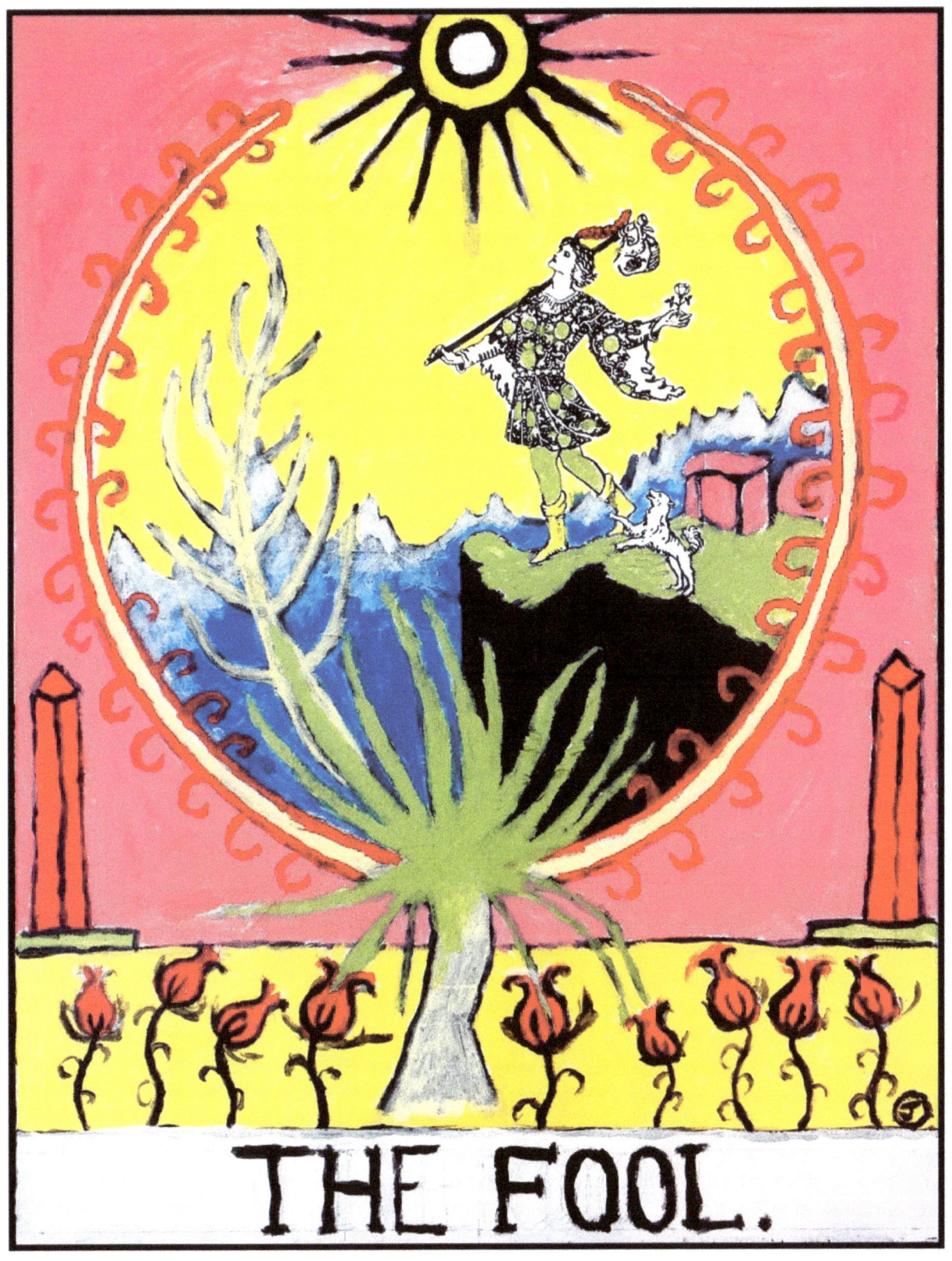

THE MAGICIAN

2015

In the collection of Elizabeth Colgrove

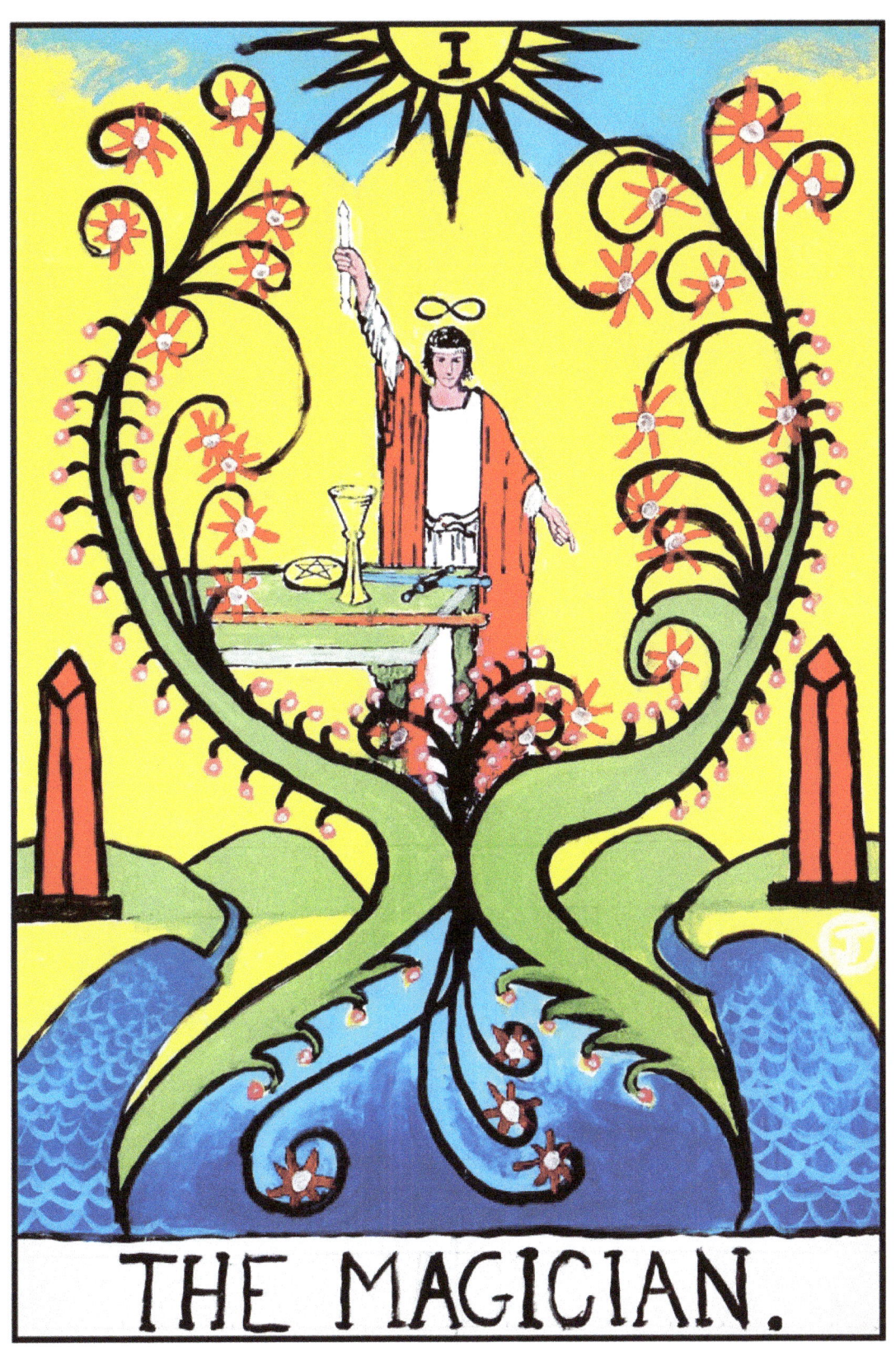

THE MAGICIAN.

THE HANGED MAN

2015

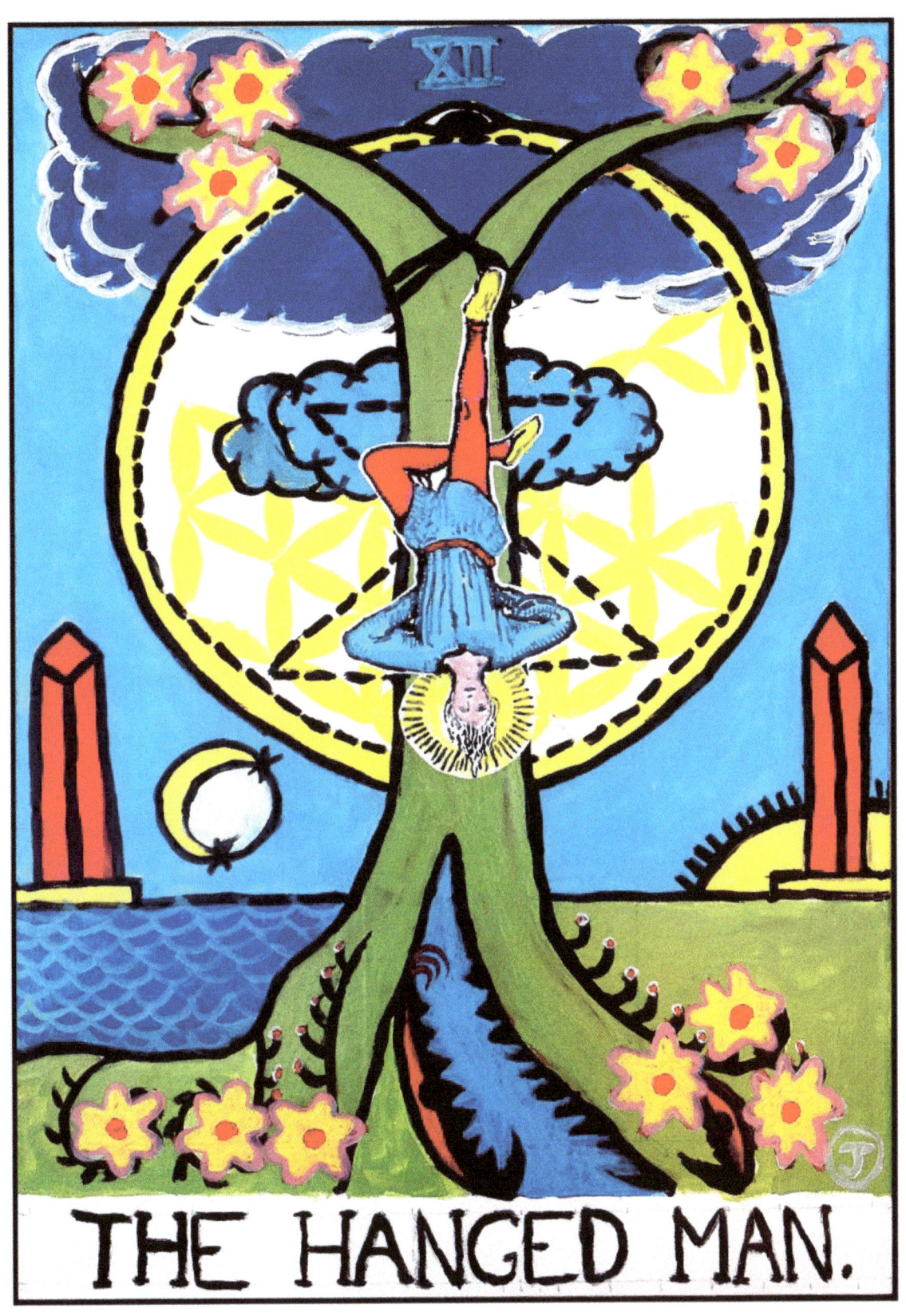

THE SUN

2015

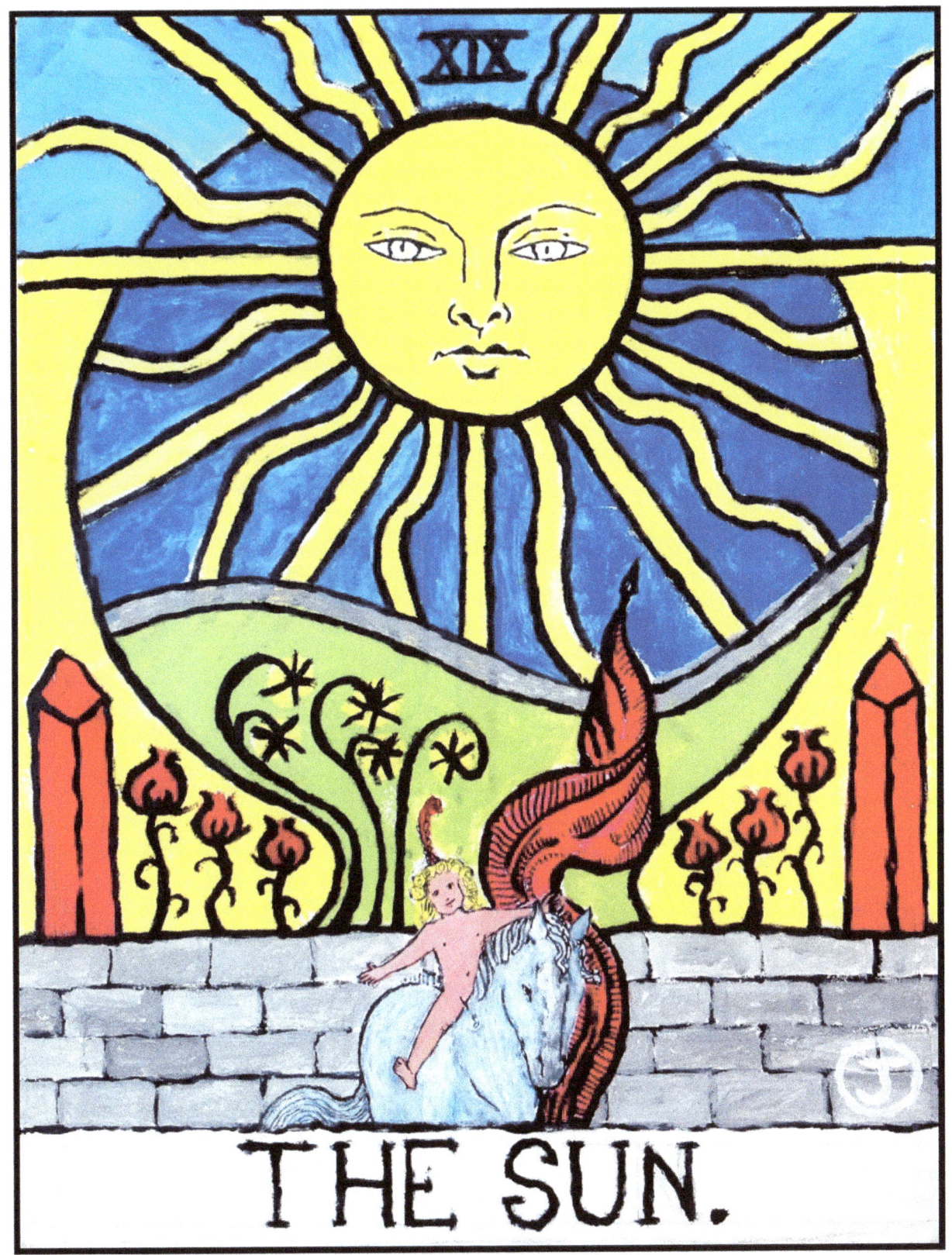

THE FOUR OF CUPS

2015

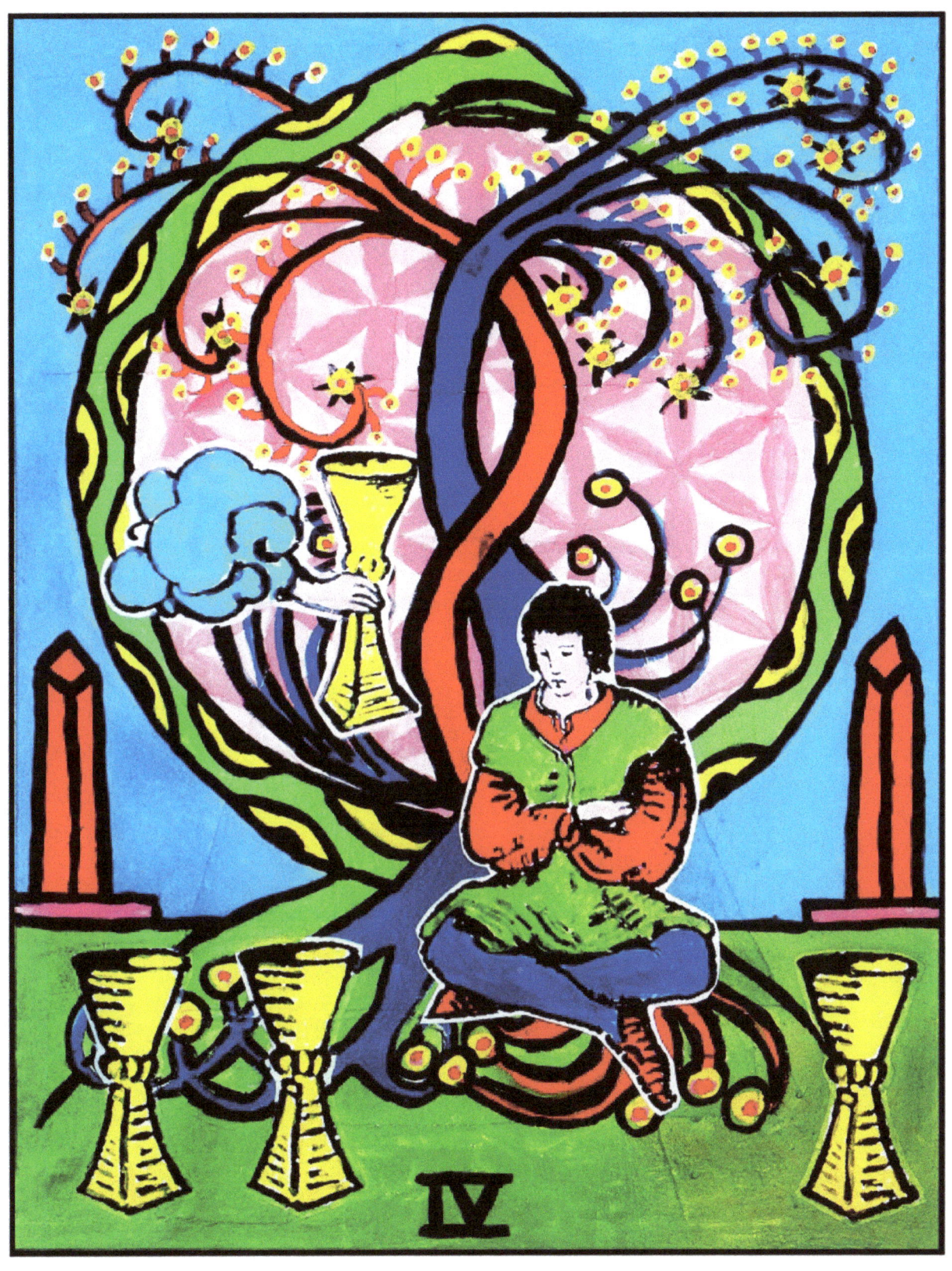

THE QUEEN OF SWORDS

2015

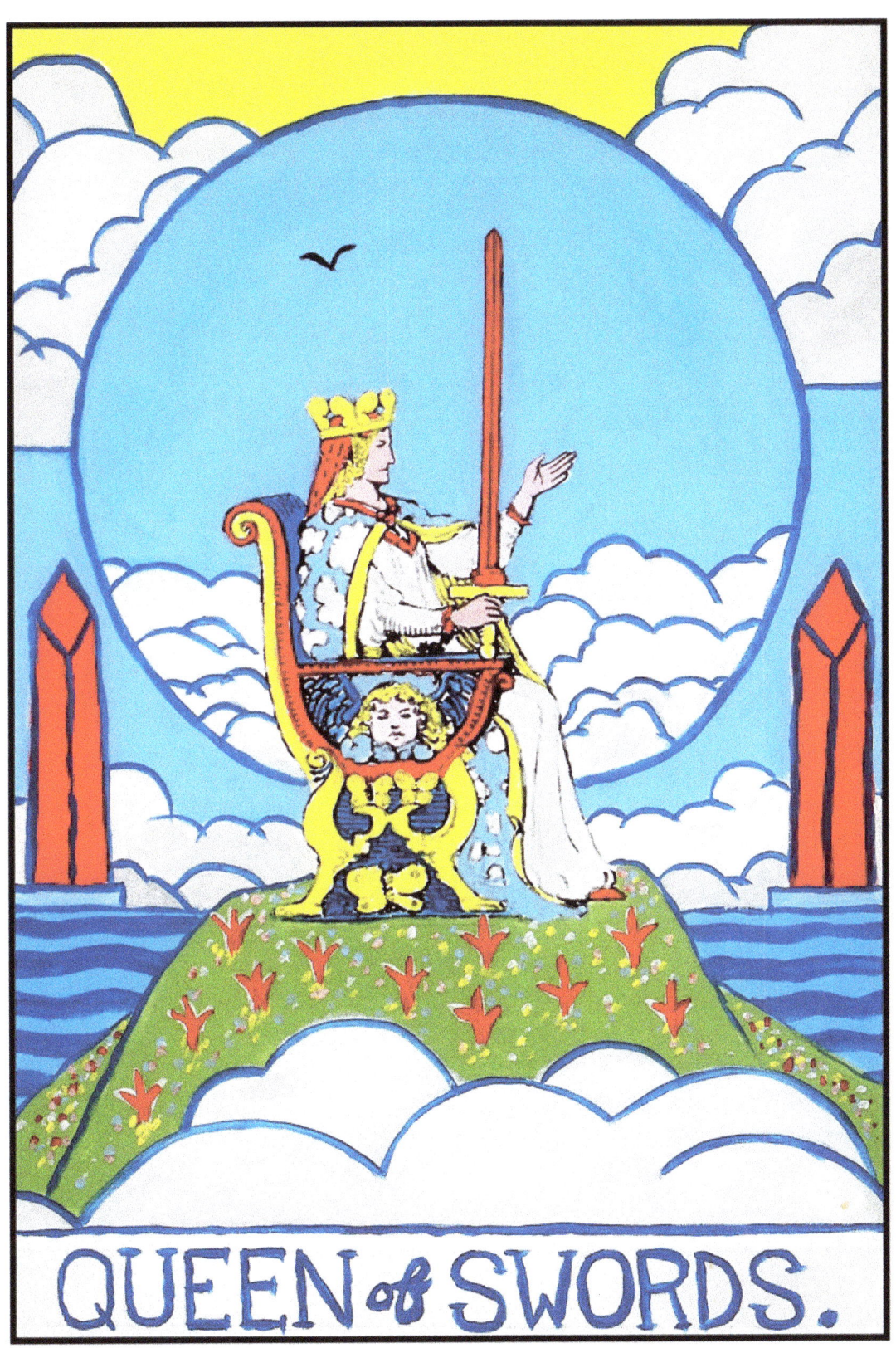

THE PAGE OF PENTACLES

2015

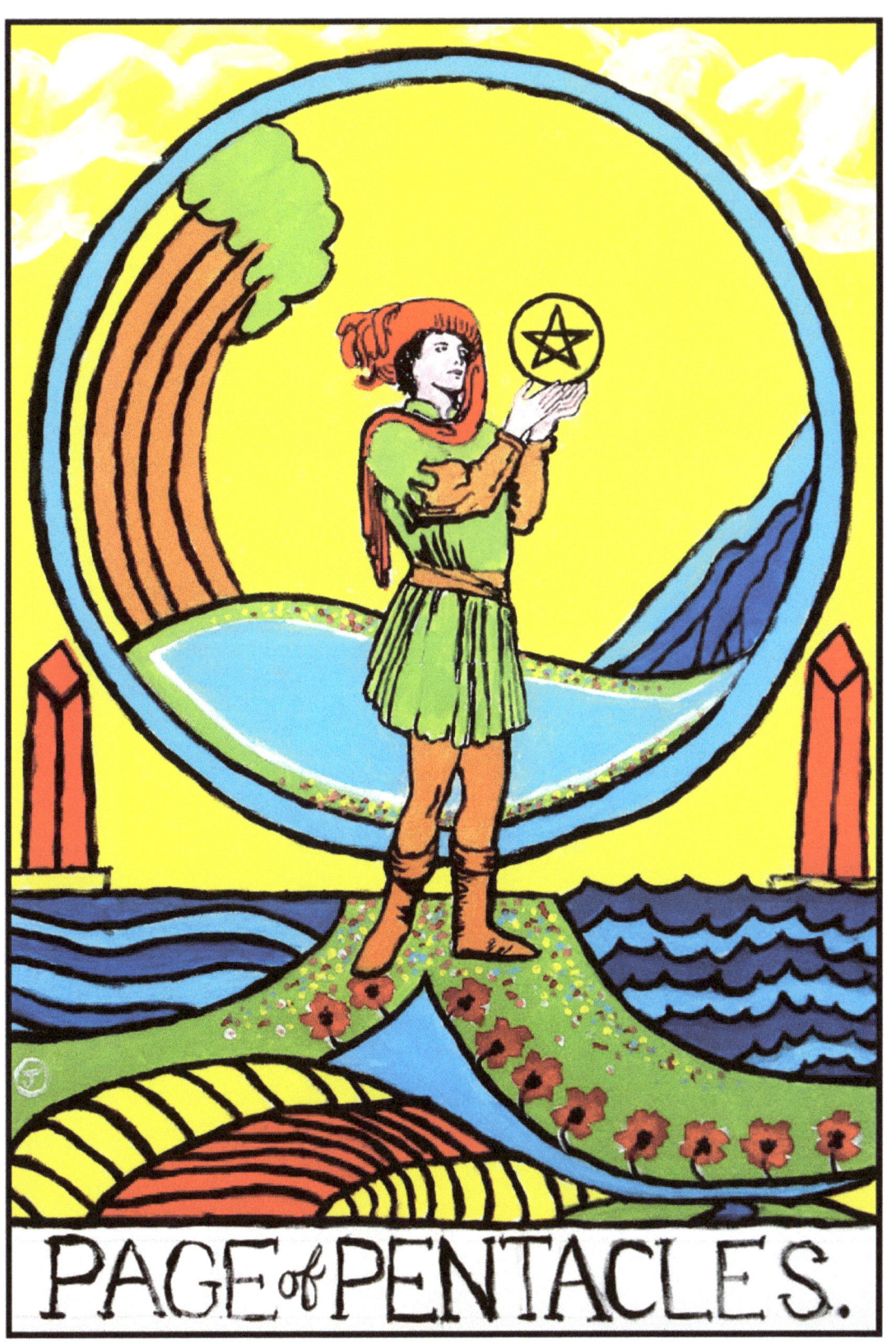

THE MOON

2015

In the collection of Ali Burton

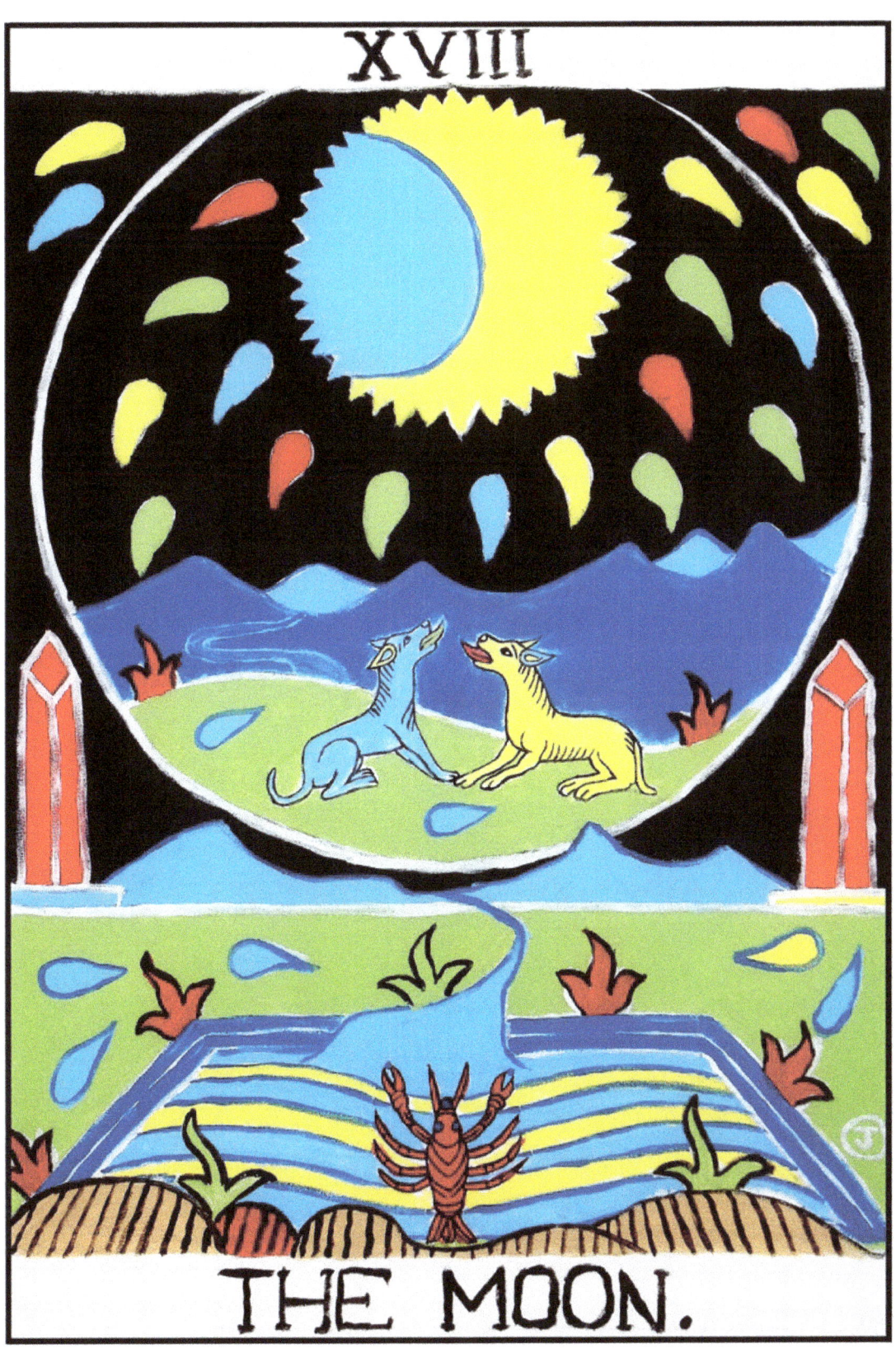

L'HERMITE

2016

In the collection of Joshua Stalskie

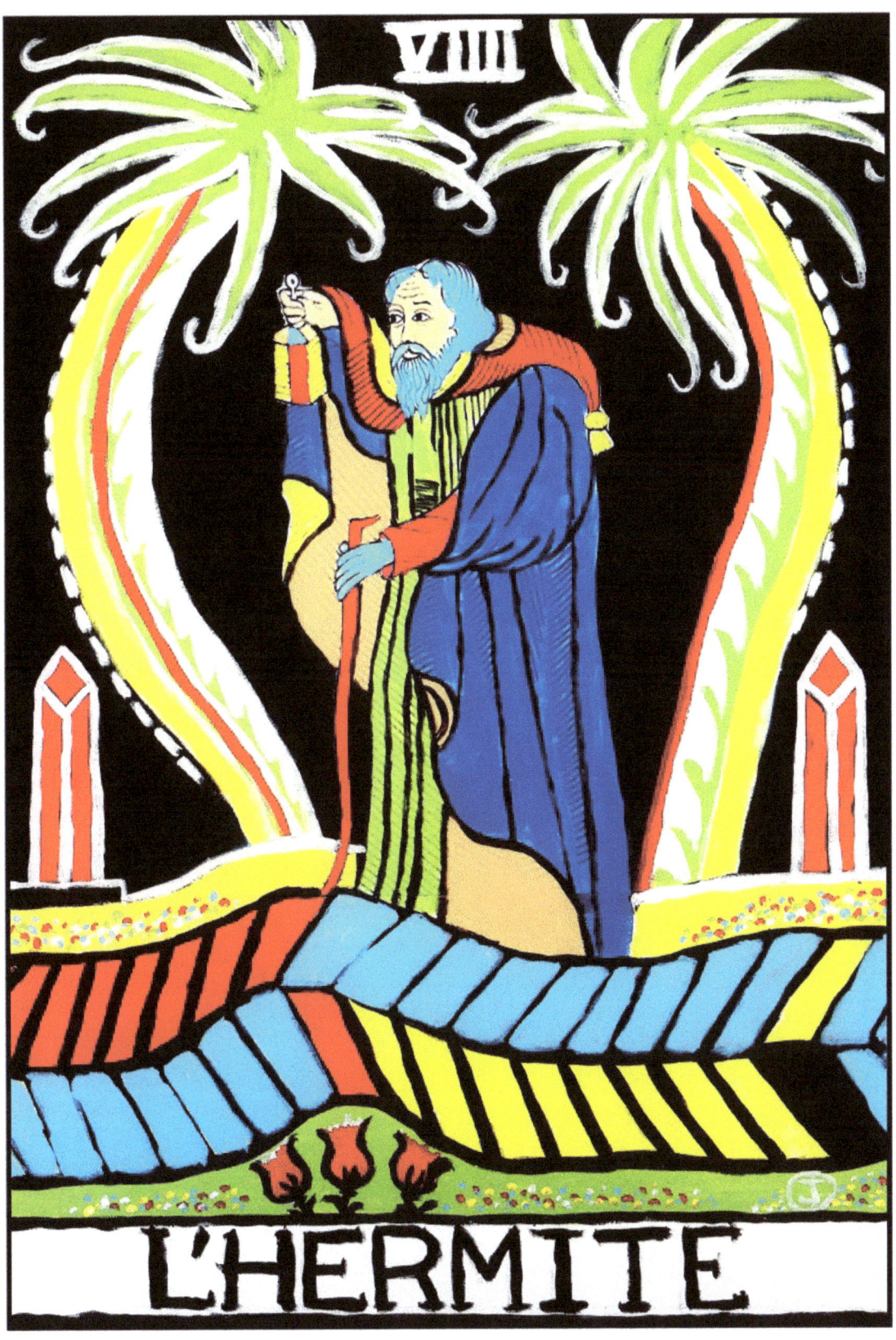

THE ACE OF CUPS

2016

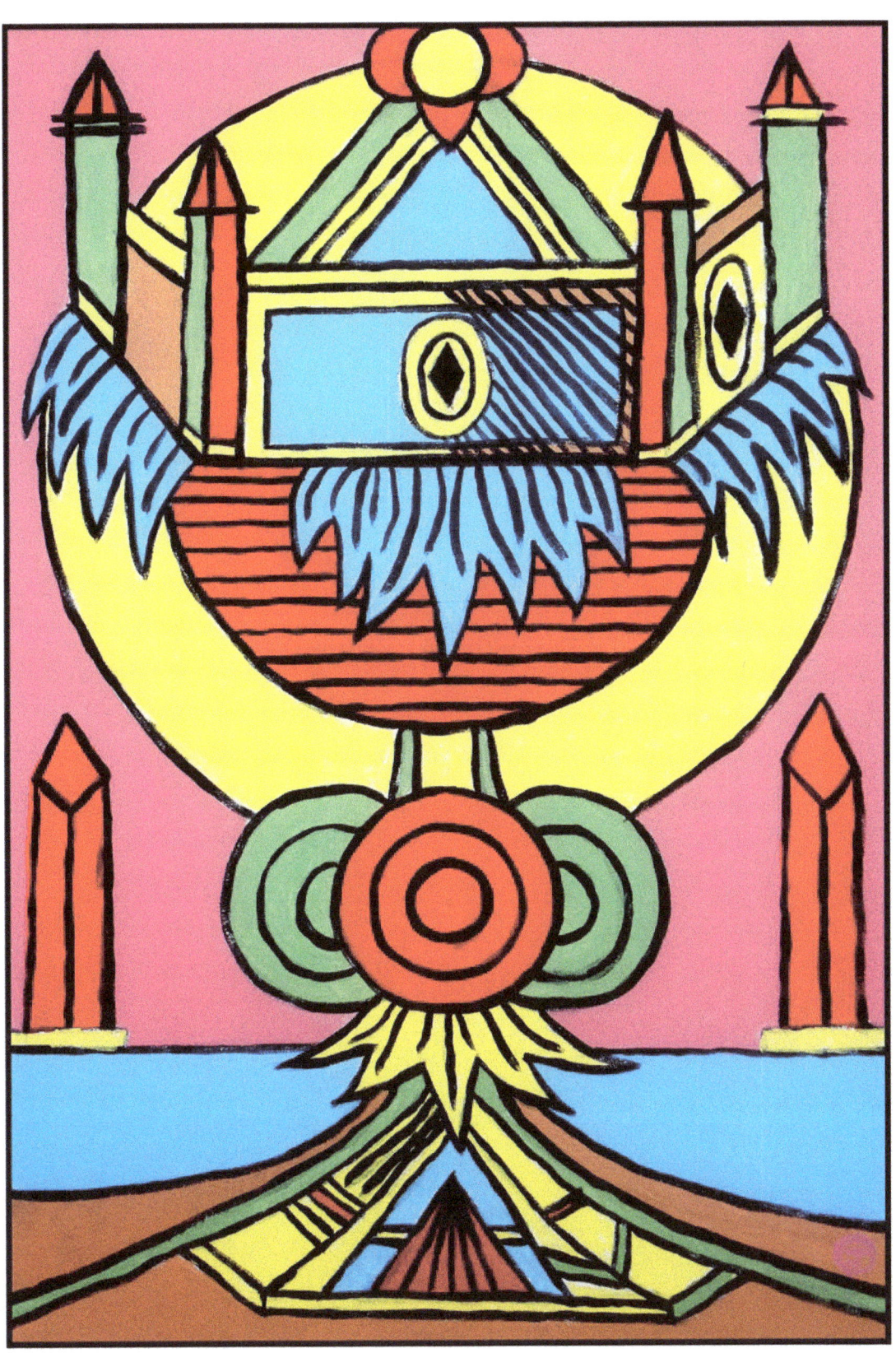

THE WORLD - CLOSED

2015

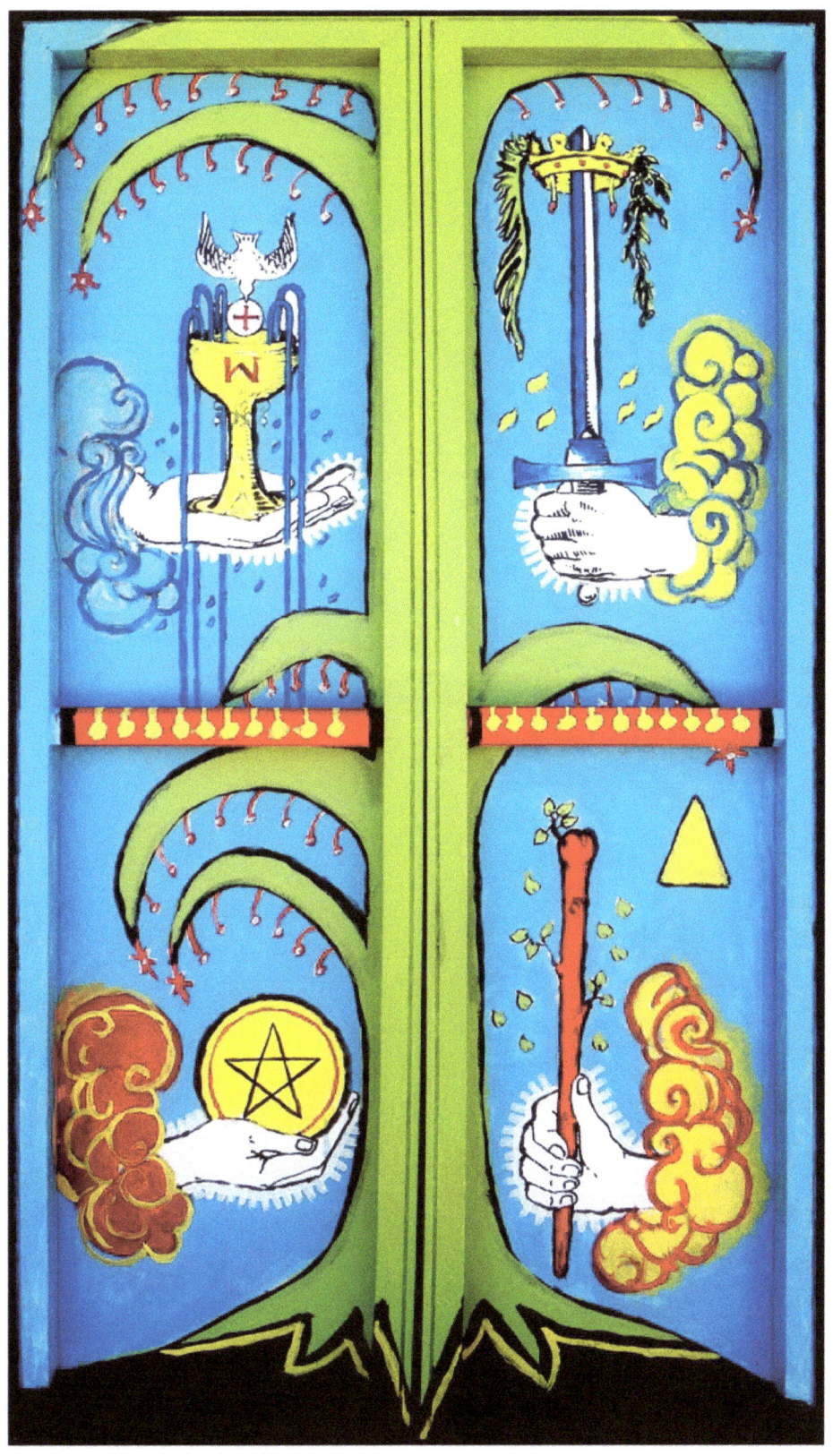

THE WORLD - OPENED

2015

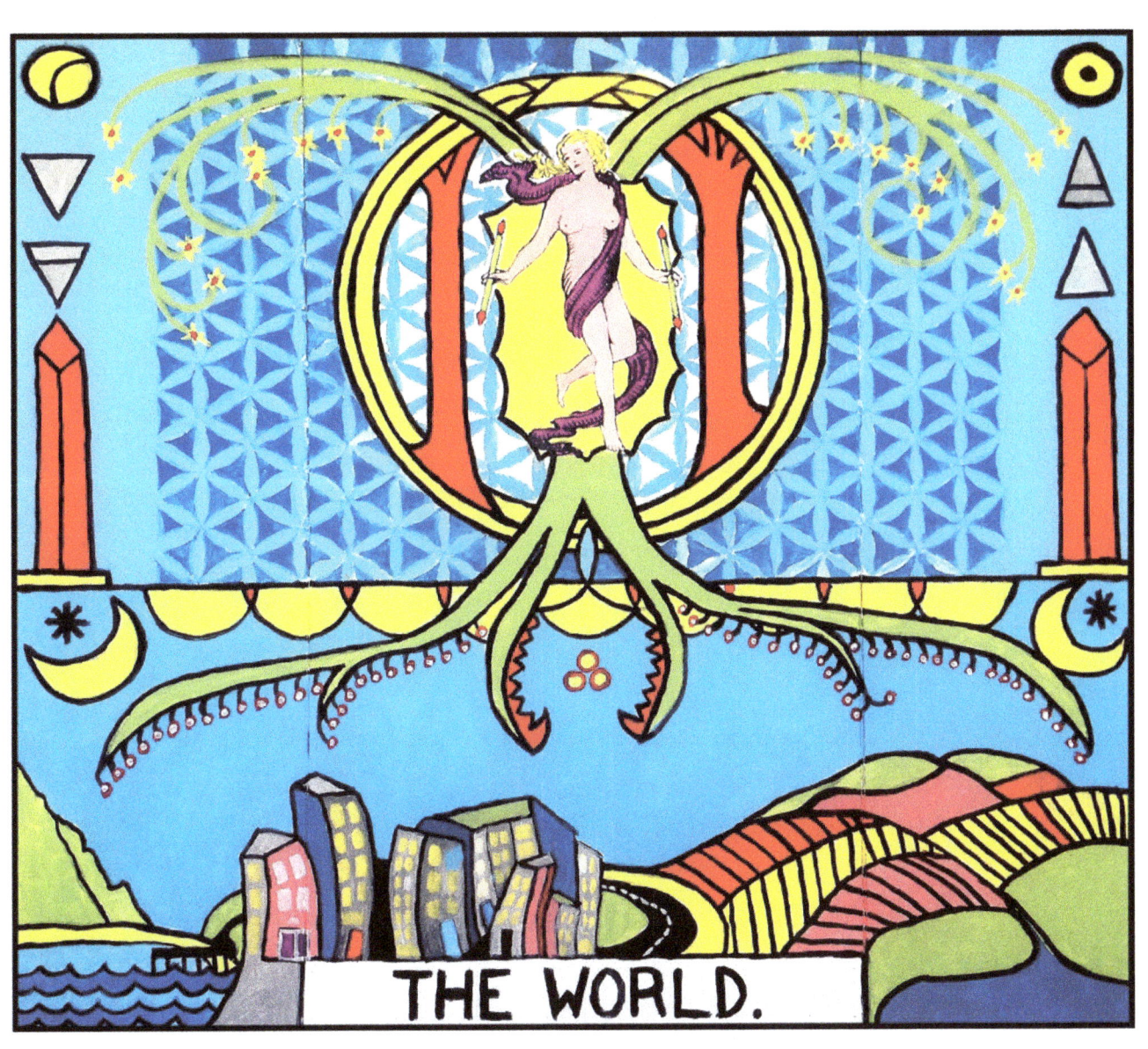

NUMBER 13

2015

In the collection of Adrienne Linn

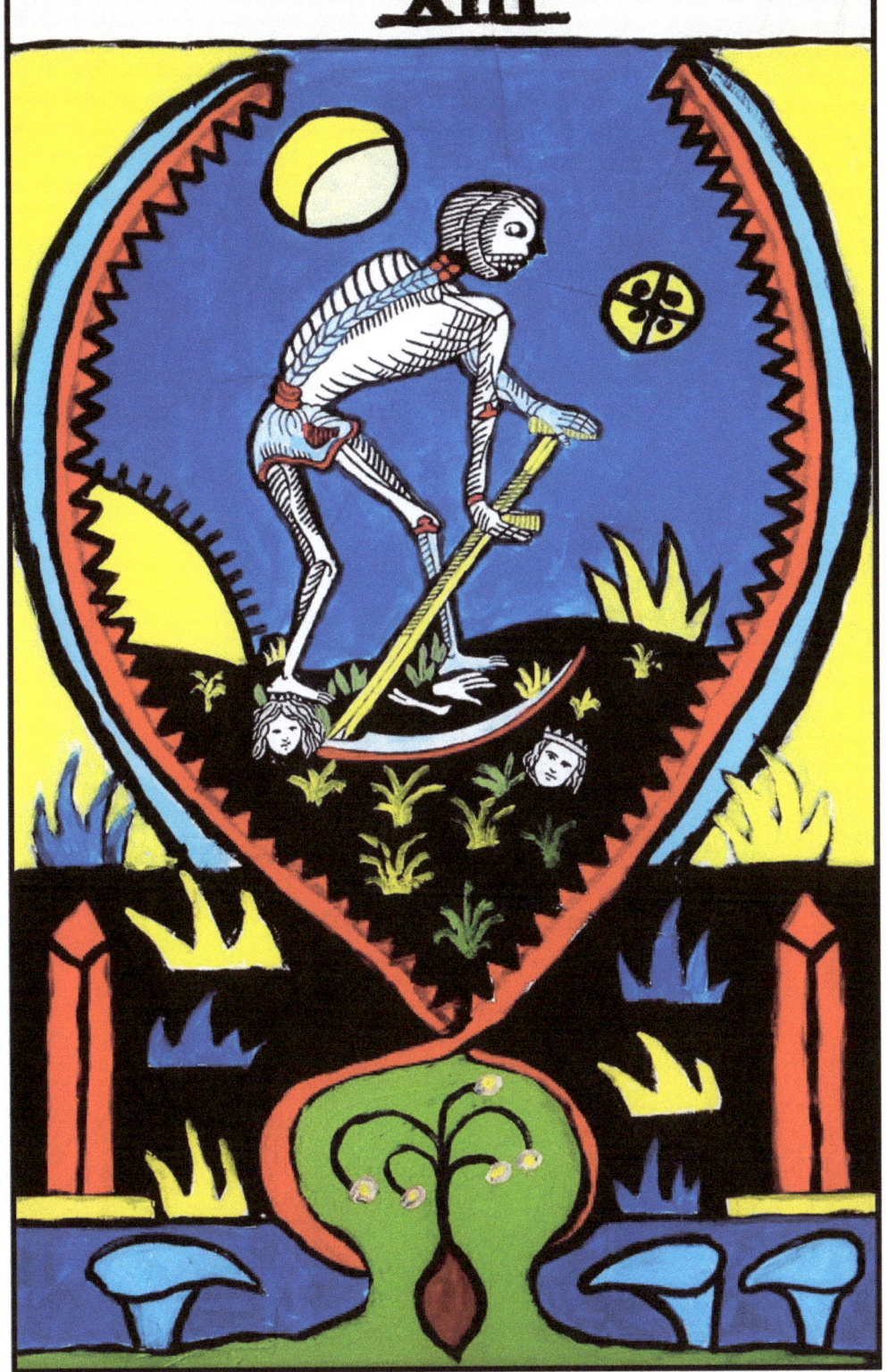

#13

2015

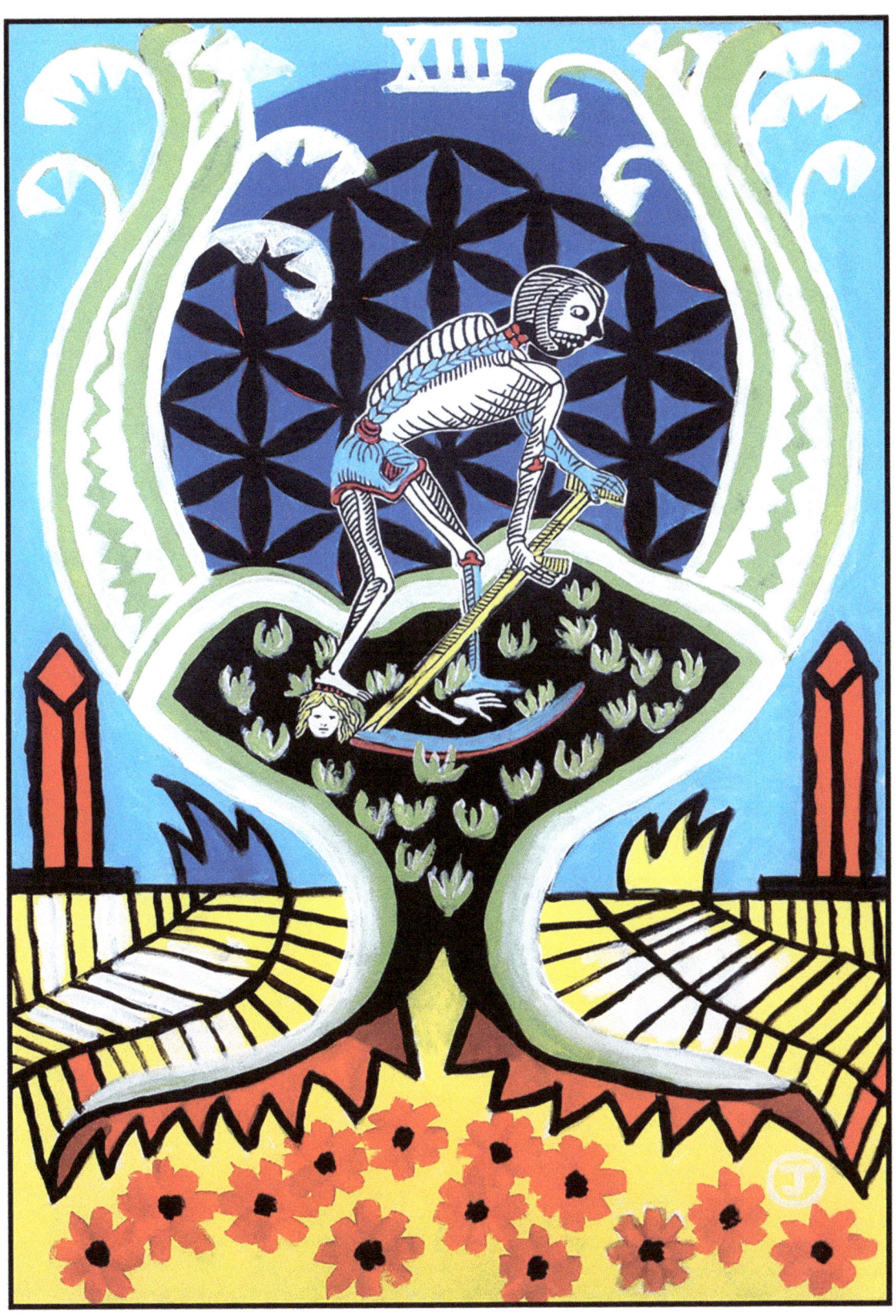

THE STAR

2015

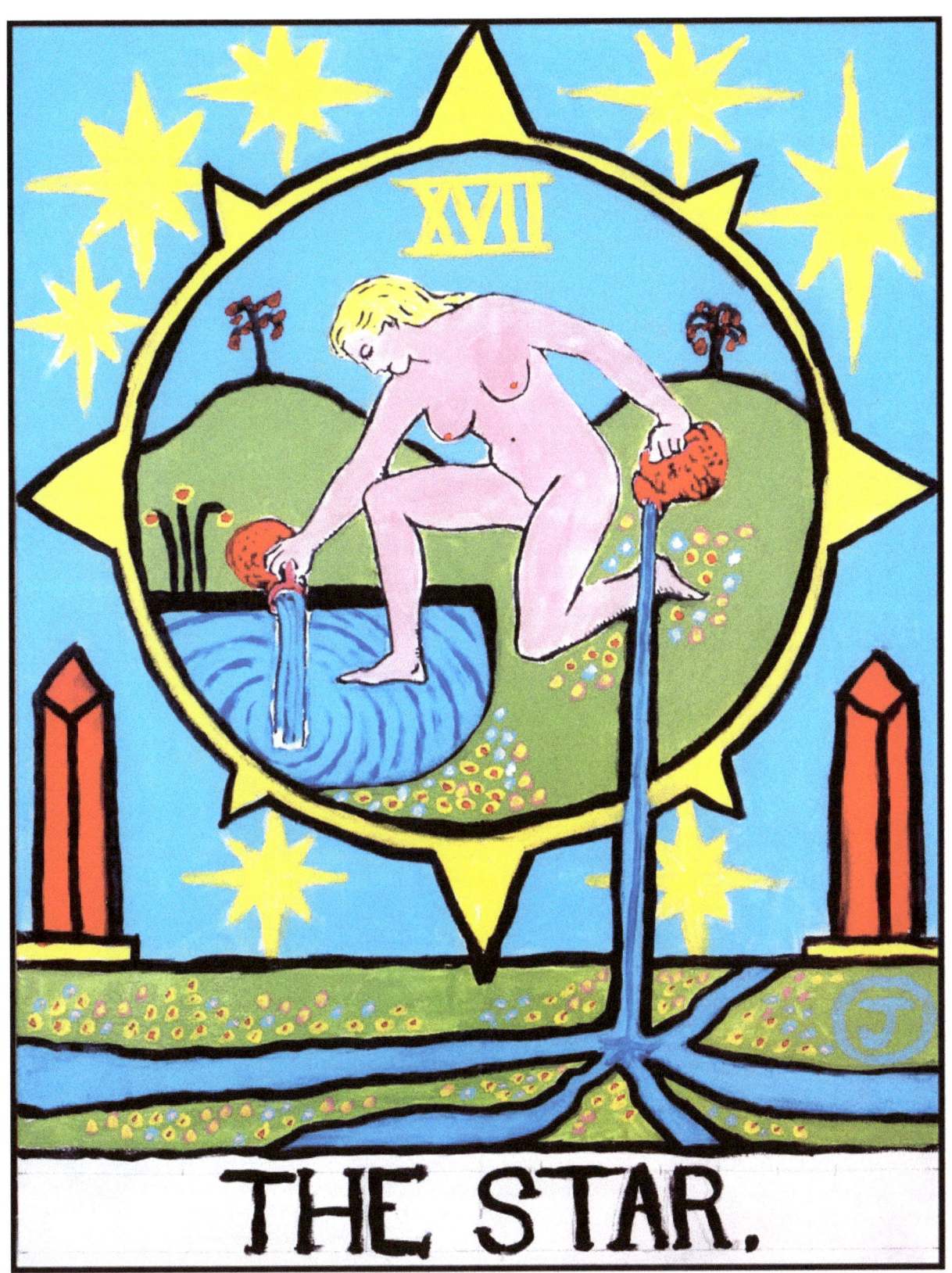

THE ACE OF PENTACLES

2016

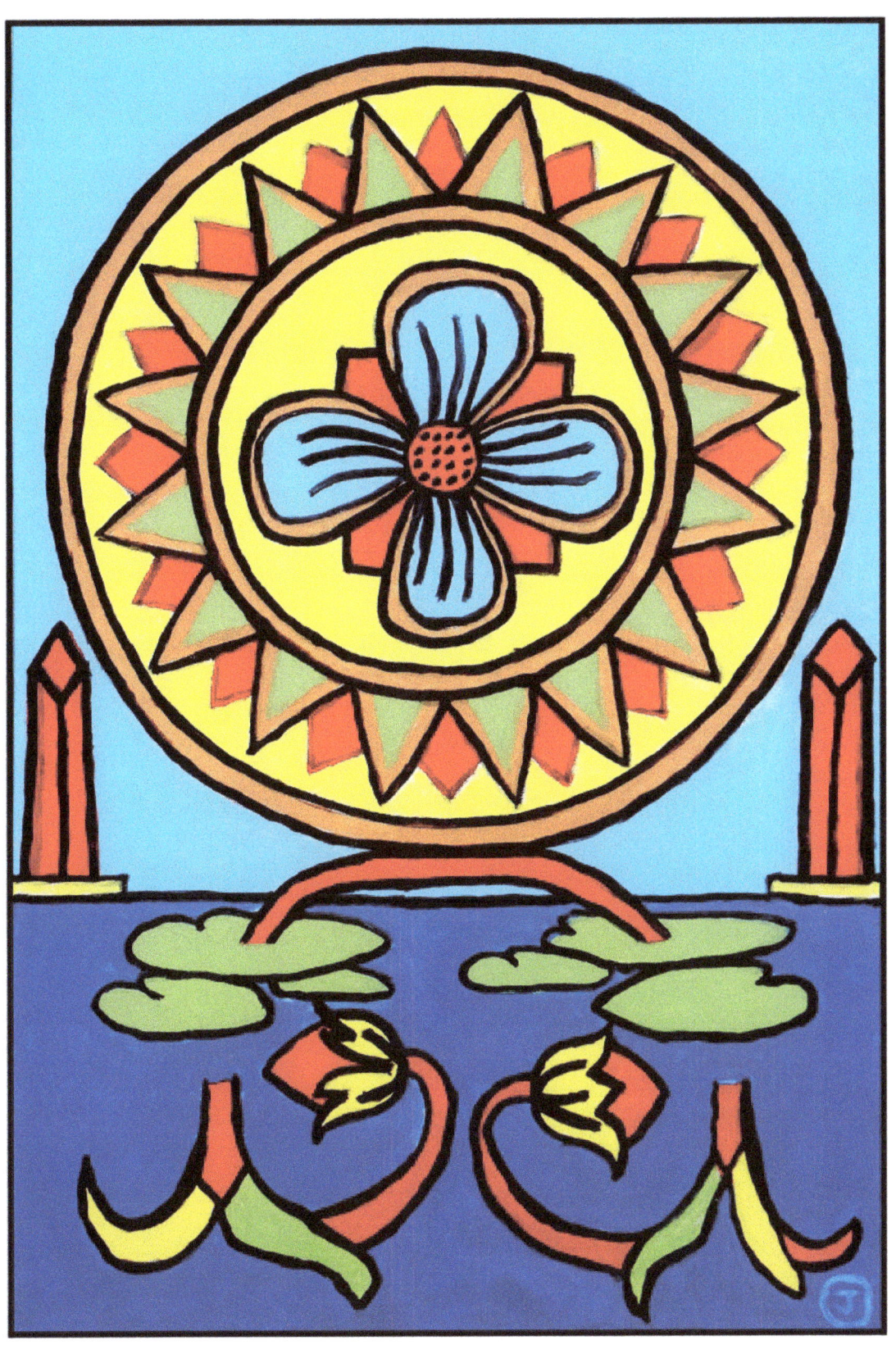

FLOWER OF LIFE - THE HEALERS

2015

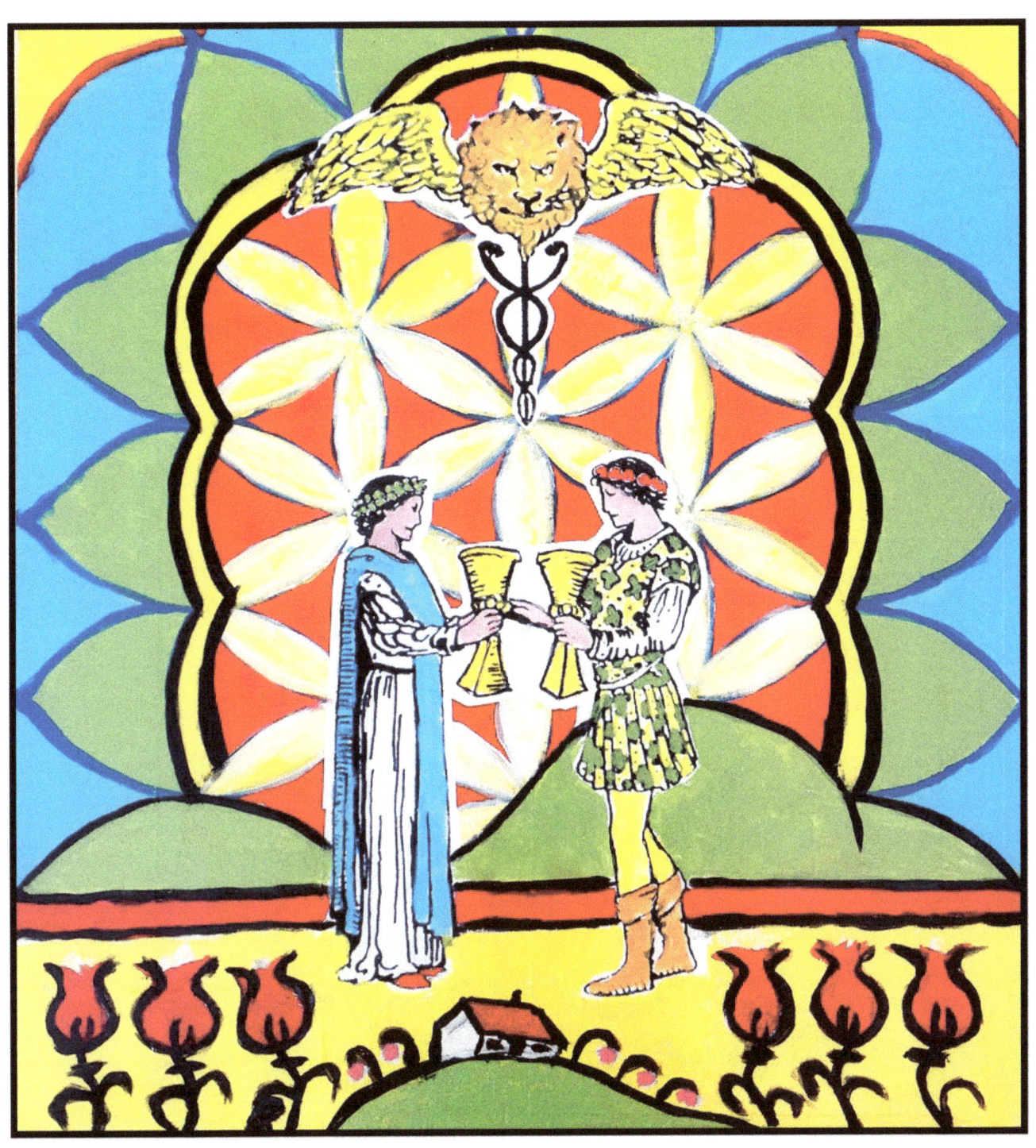

THE FLOWER OF LIFE - AS ABOVE SO BELOW

2015

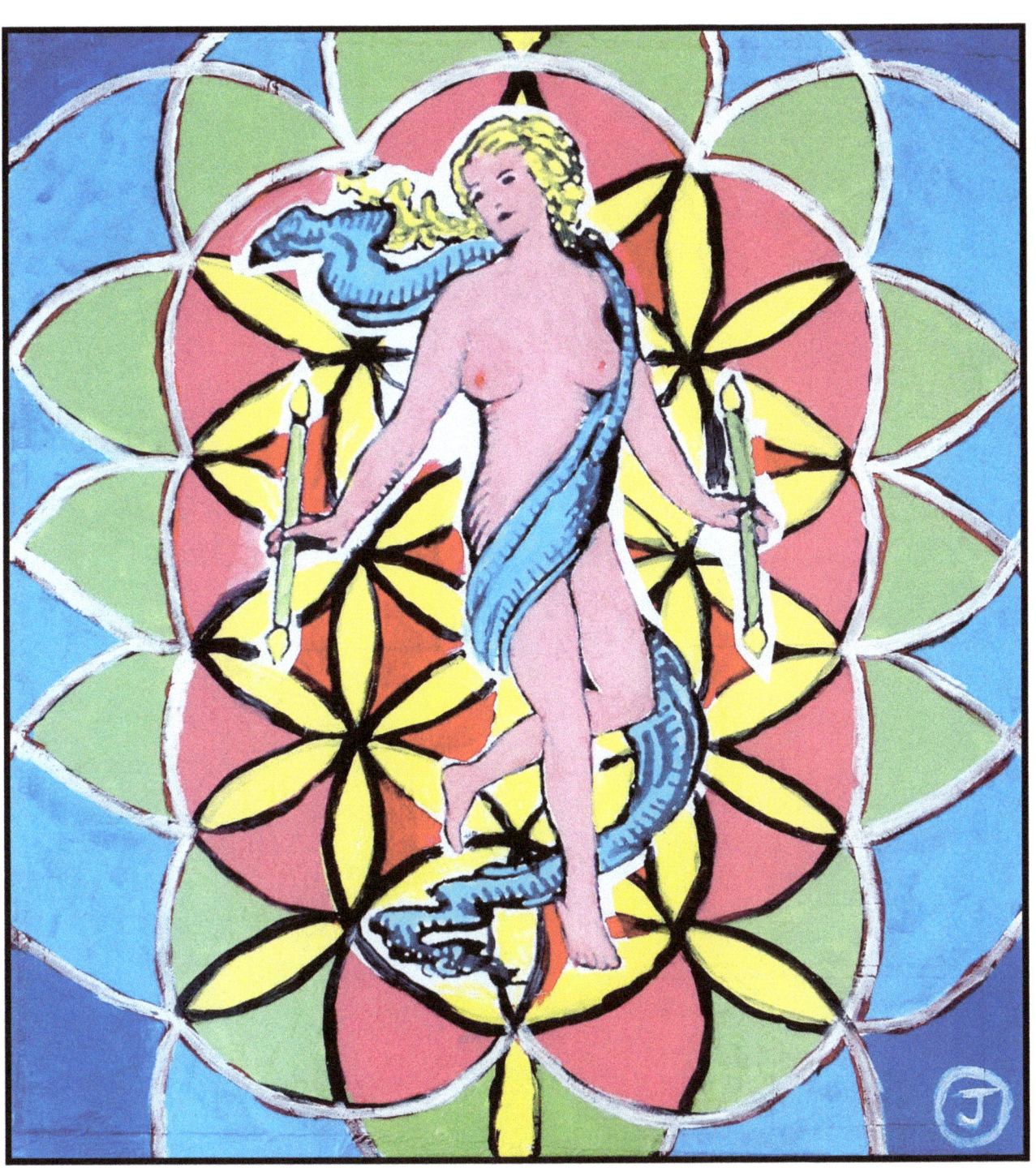

THE MYSTERY OF THE HOLY GRAIL

2016

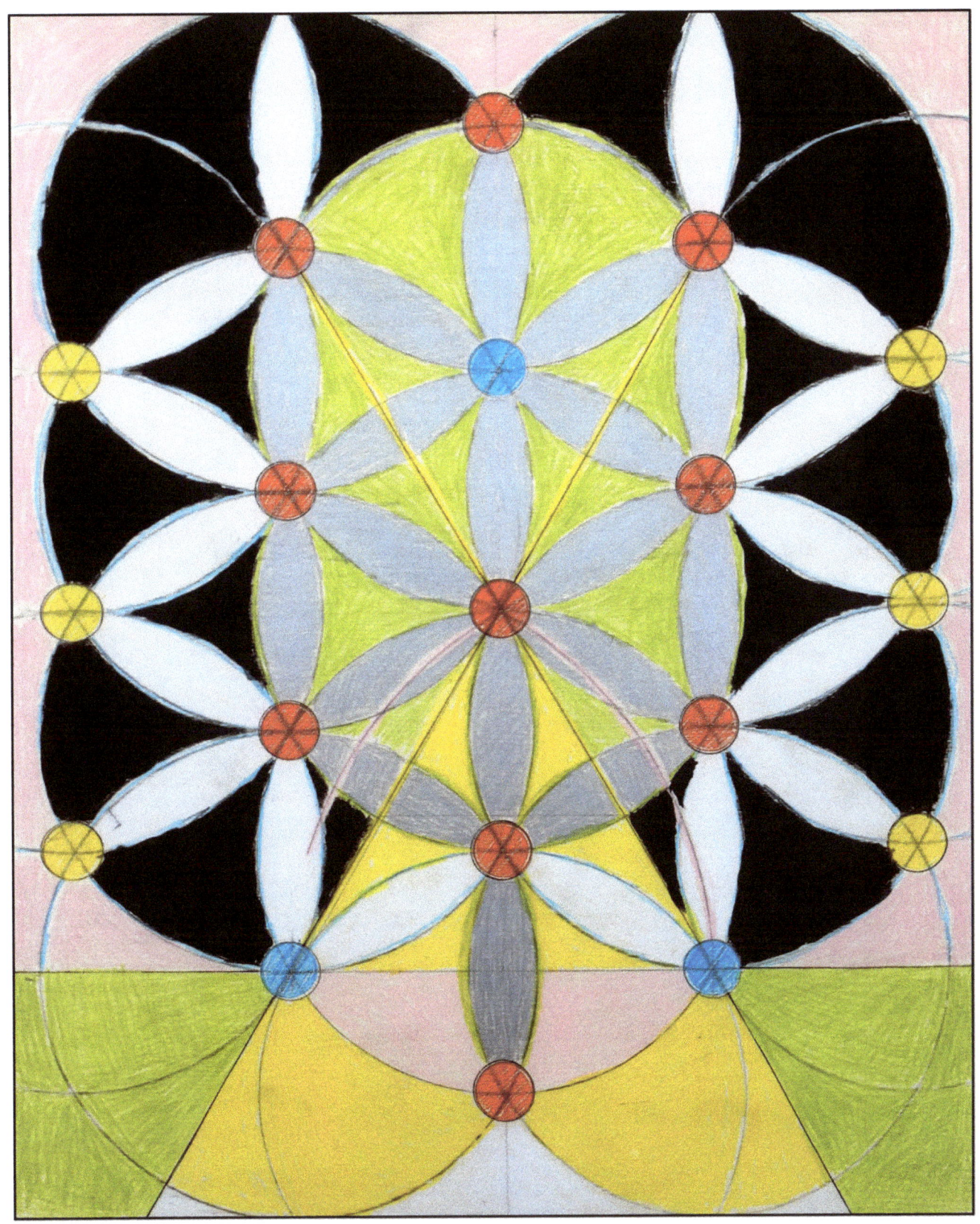

LIFE IN THE MICROCOSM

2016

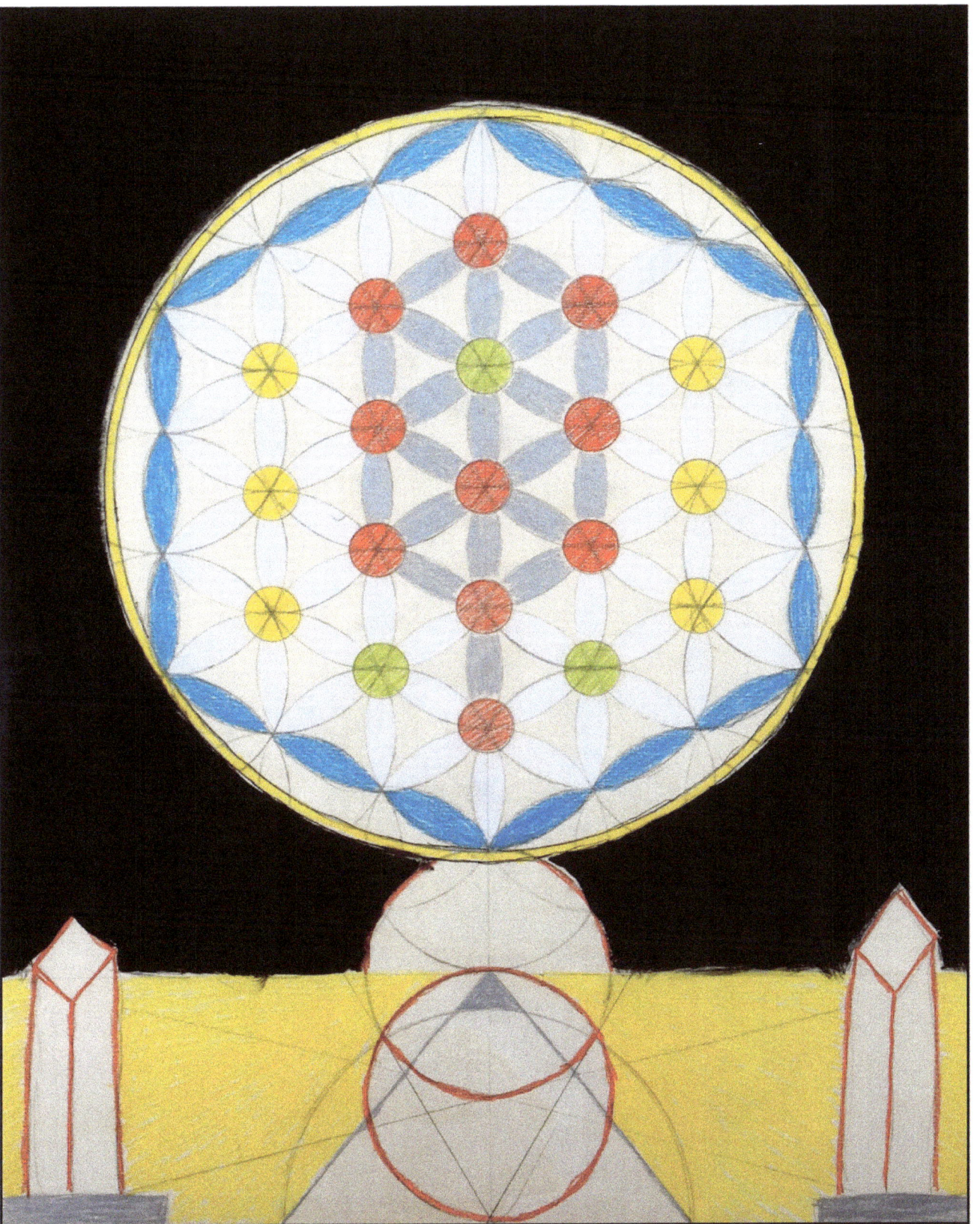

THE CAT'S CRADLE

2016

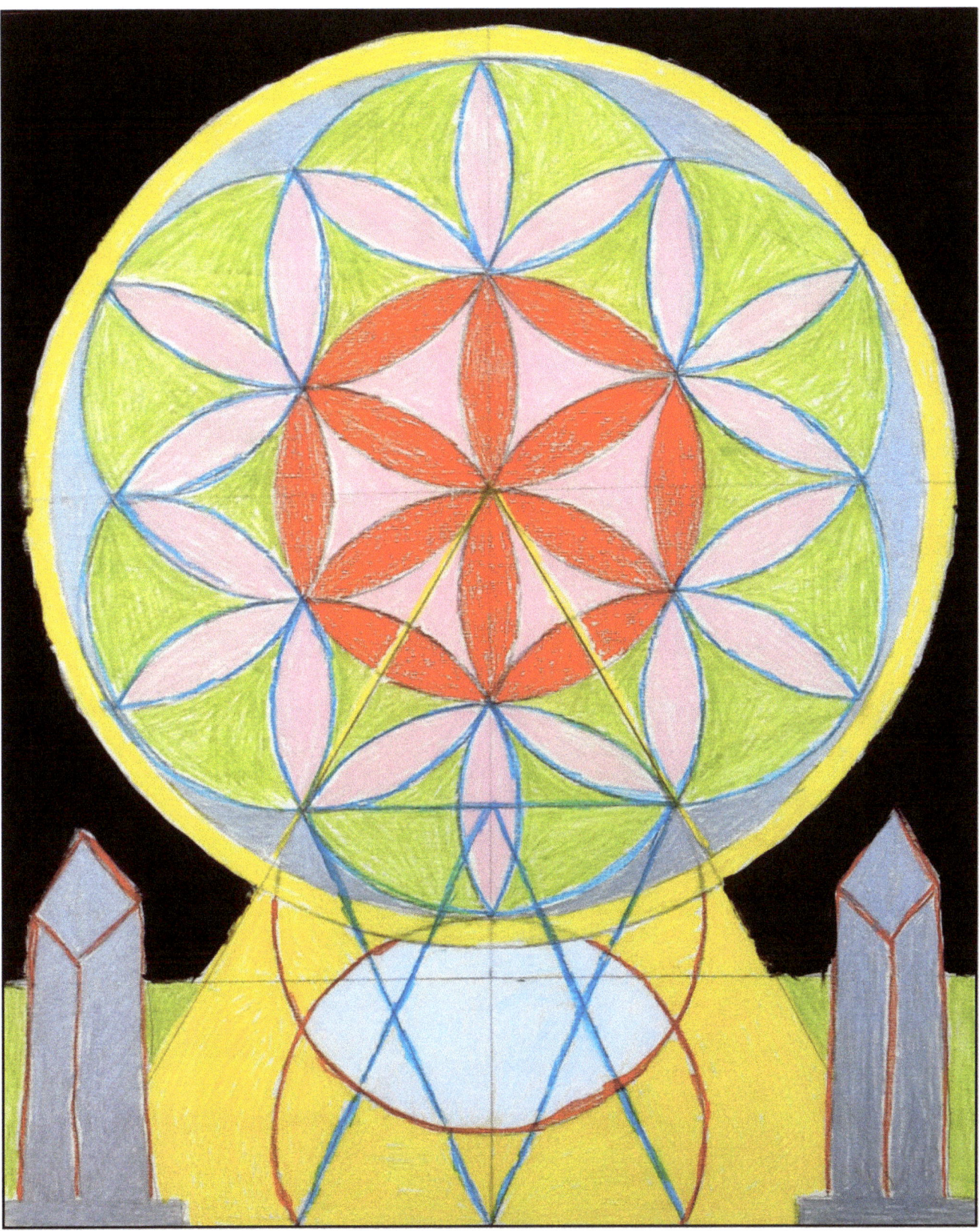

THE FRUIT OF LIFE

2016

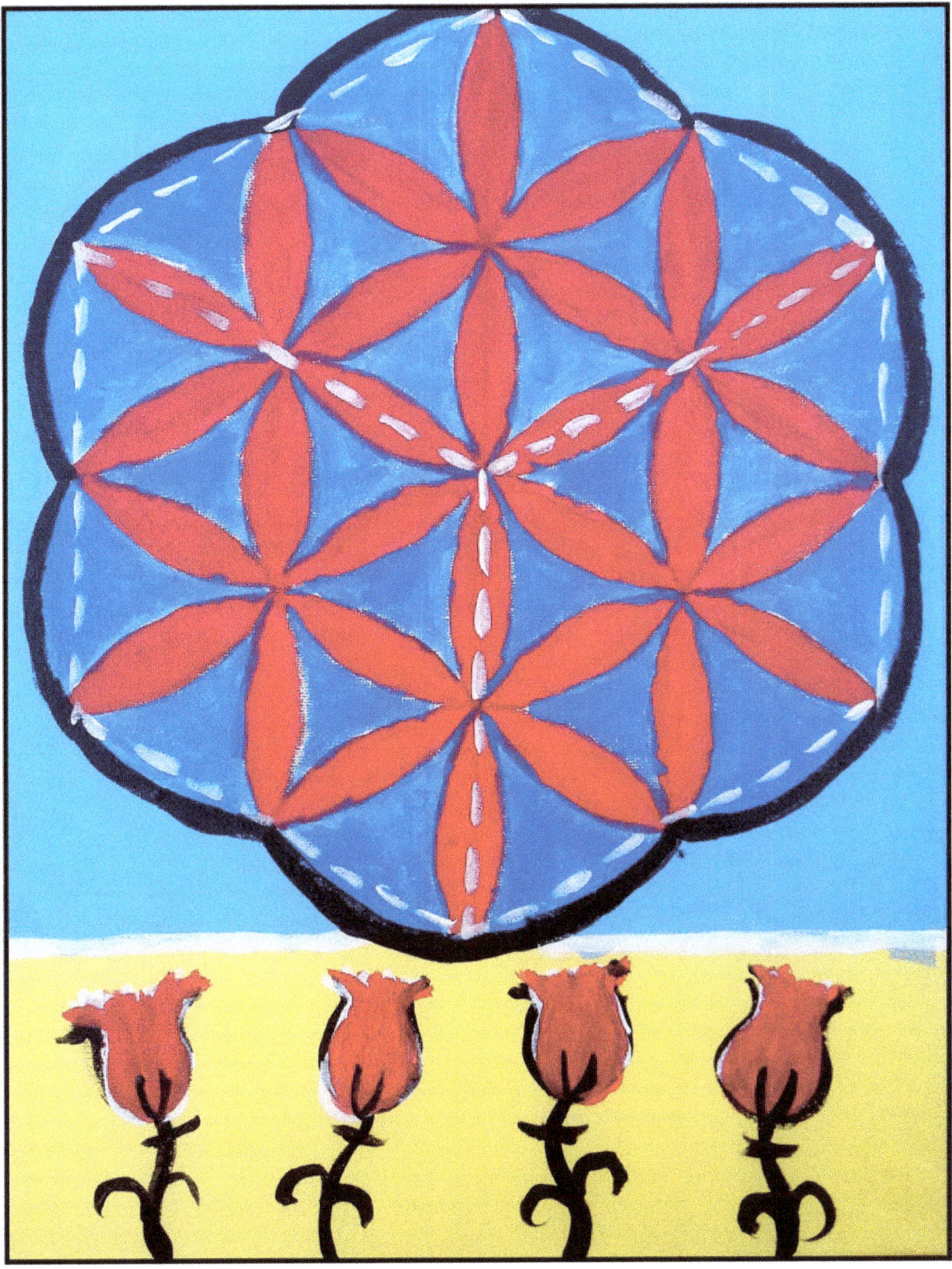

THE LADDER TO THE HEAVENS NOW

2016

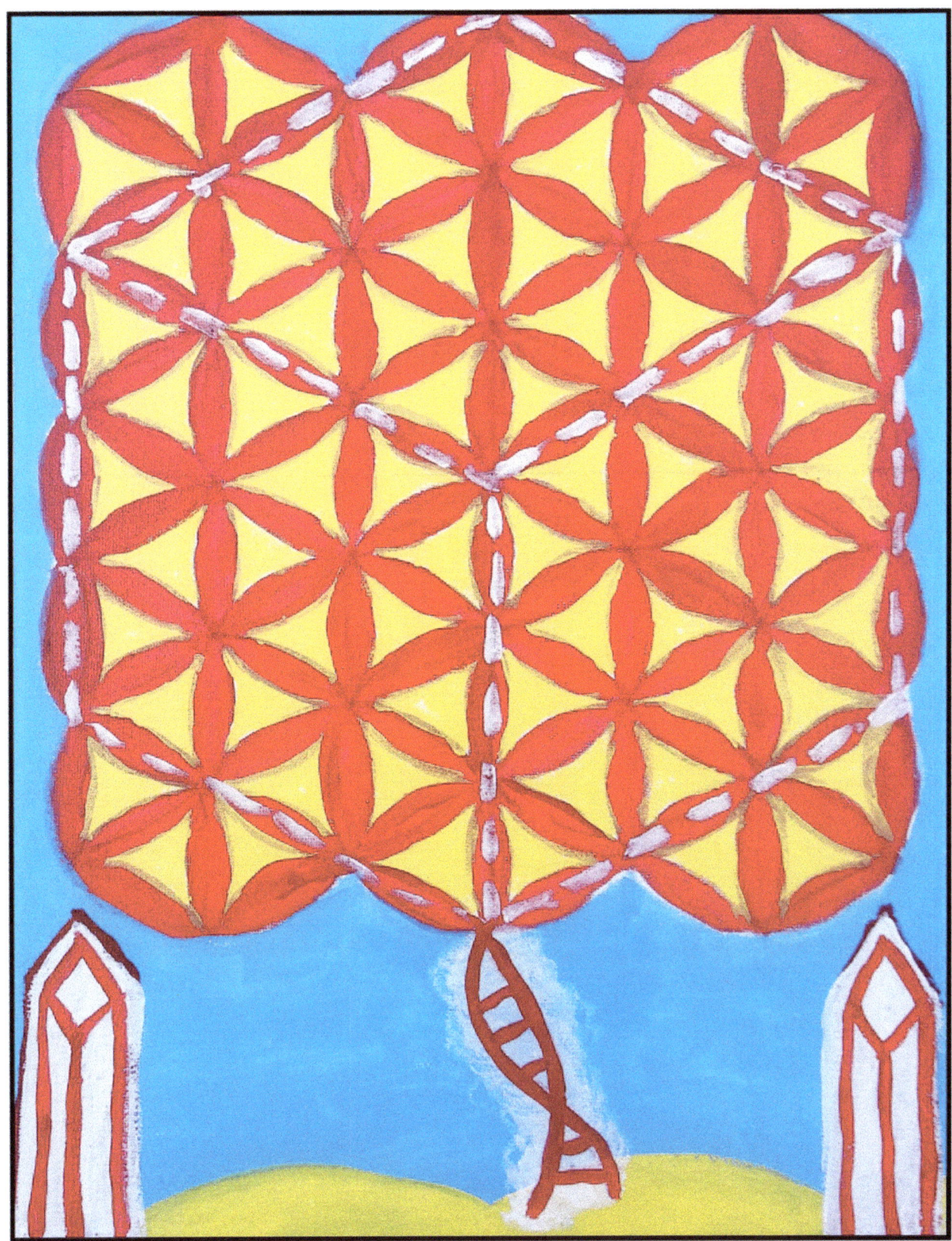

THE SEED OF LIFE

2016

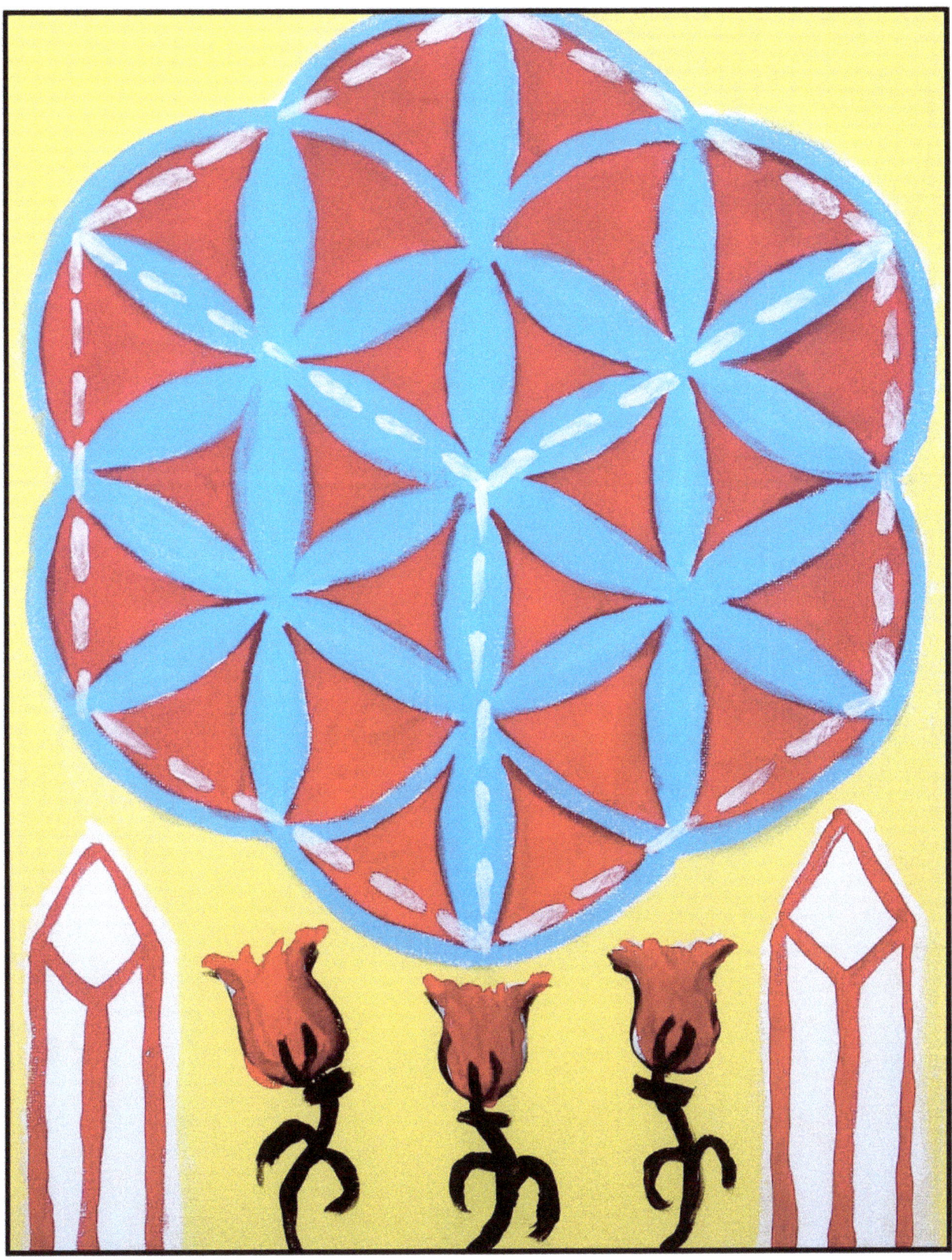

MANUFACTURING REALITY IN AN UPSIDE-DOWN WORLD

2016

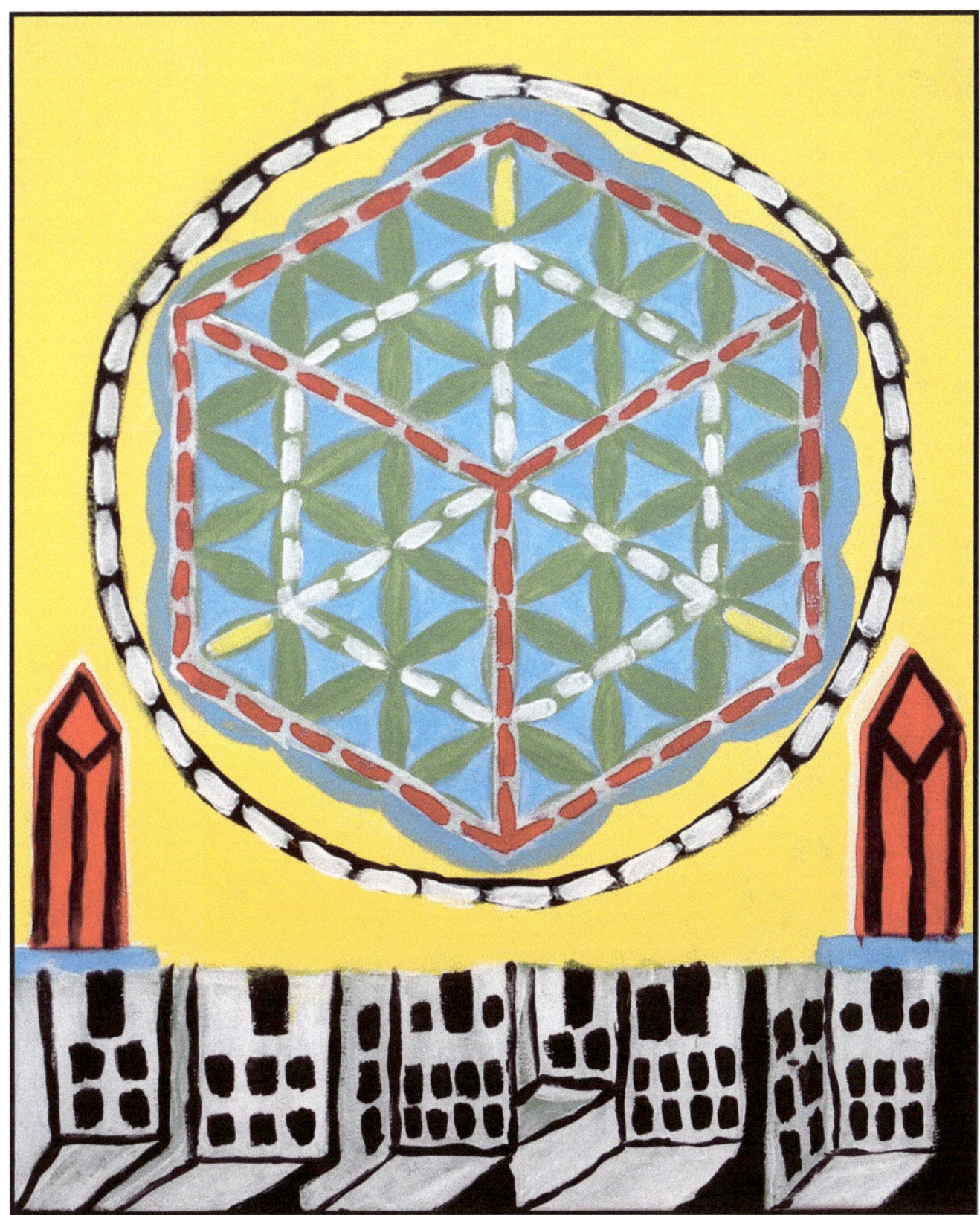

SEFIROT

2016

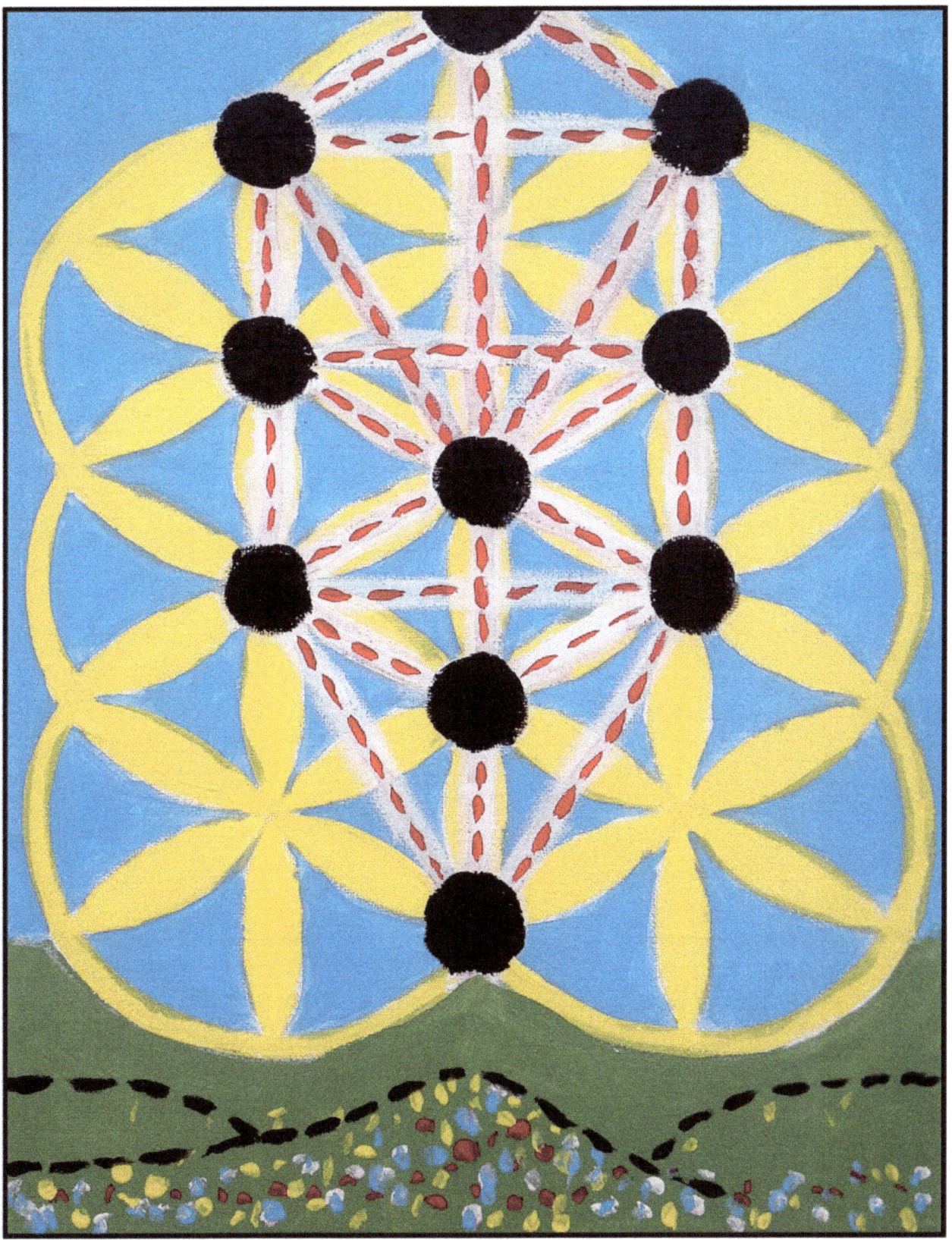

A POINT OF ATTENTION IN AN UPSIDE-DOWN WORLD

2016

In the collection of Ali Burton

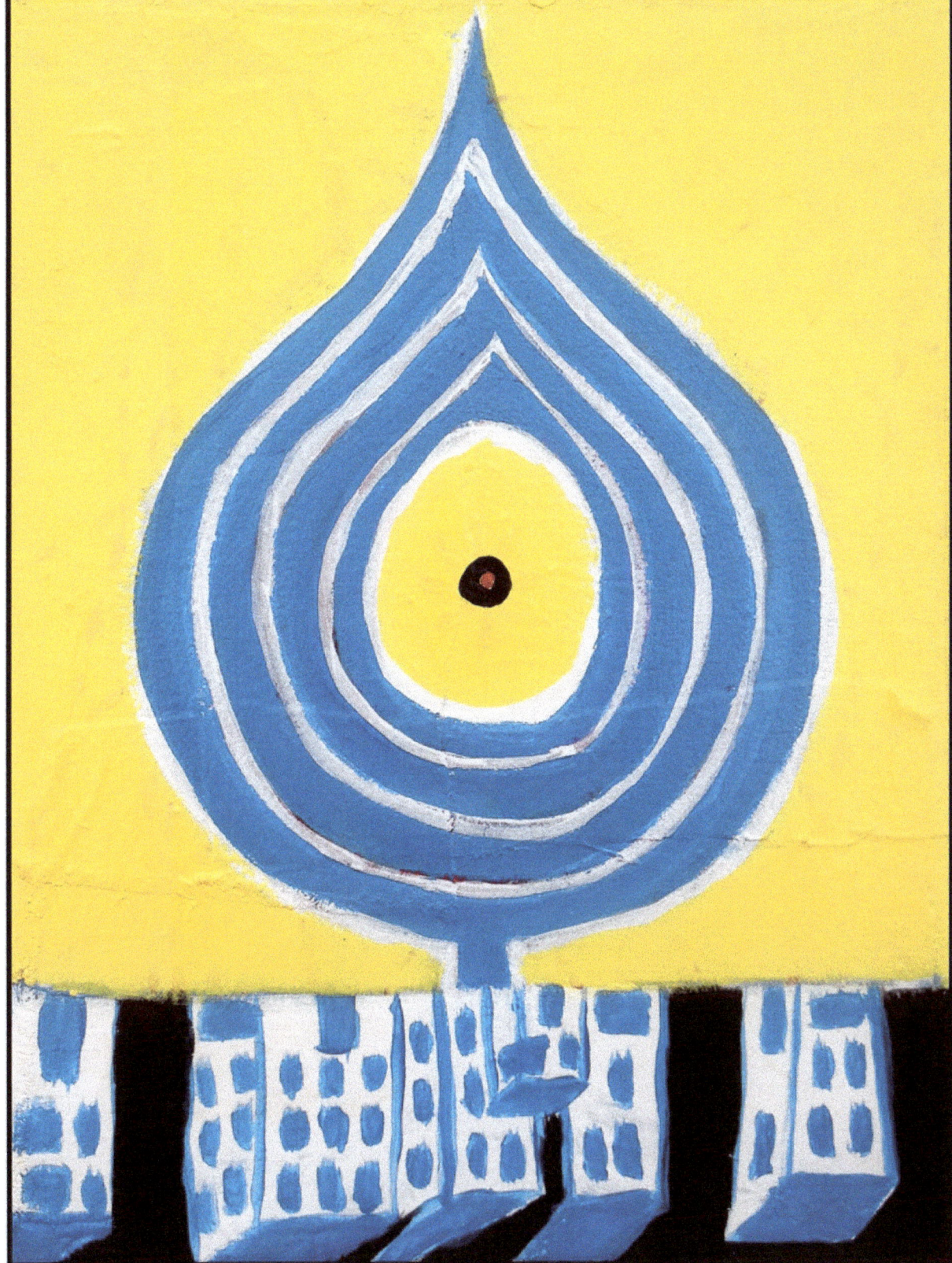

THE PYRAMID OF THE MOON

2016

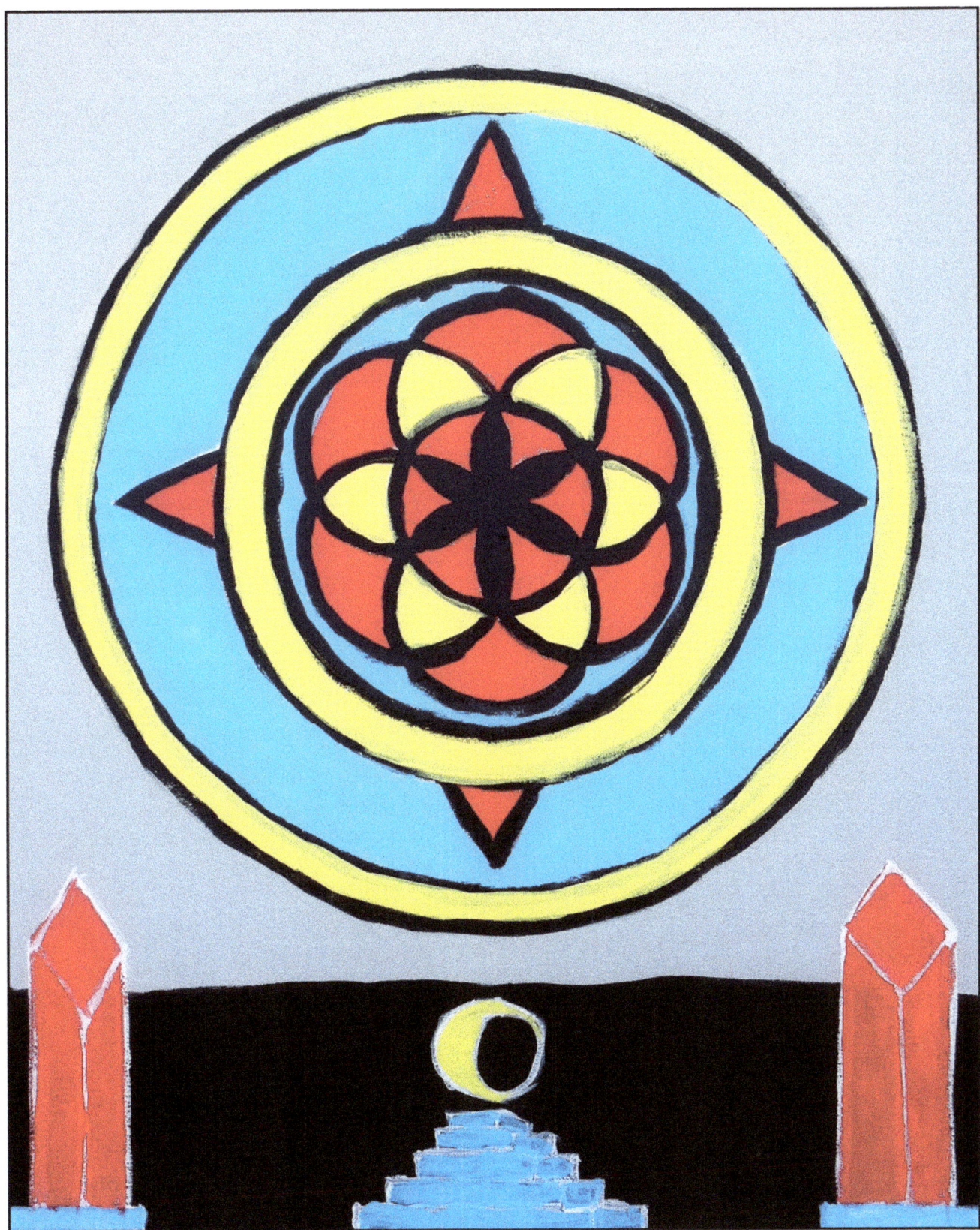

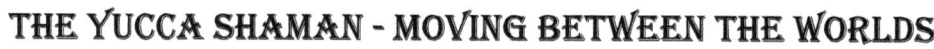

THE YUCCA SHAMAN - MOVING BETWEEN THE WORLDS

2016

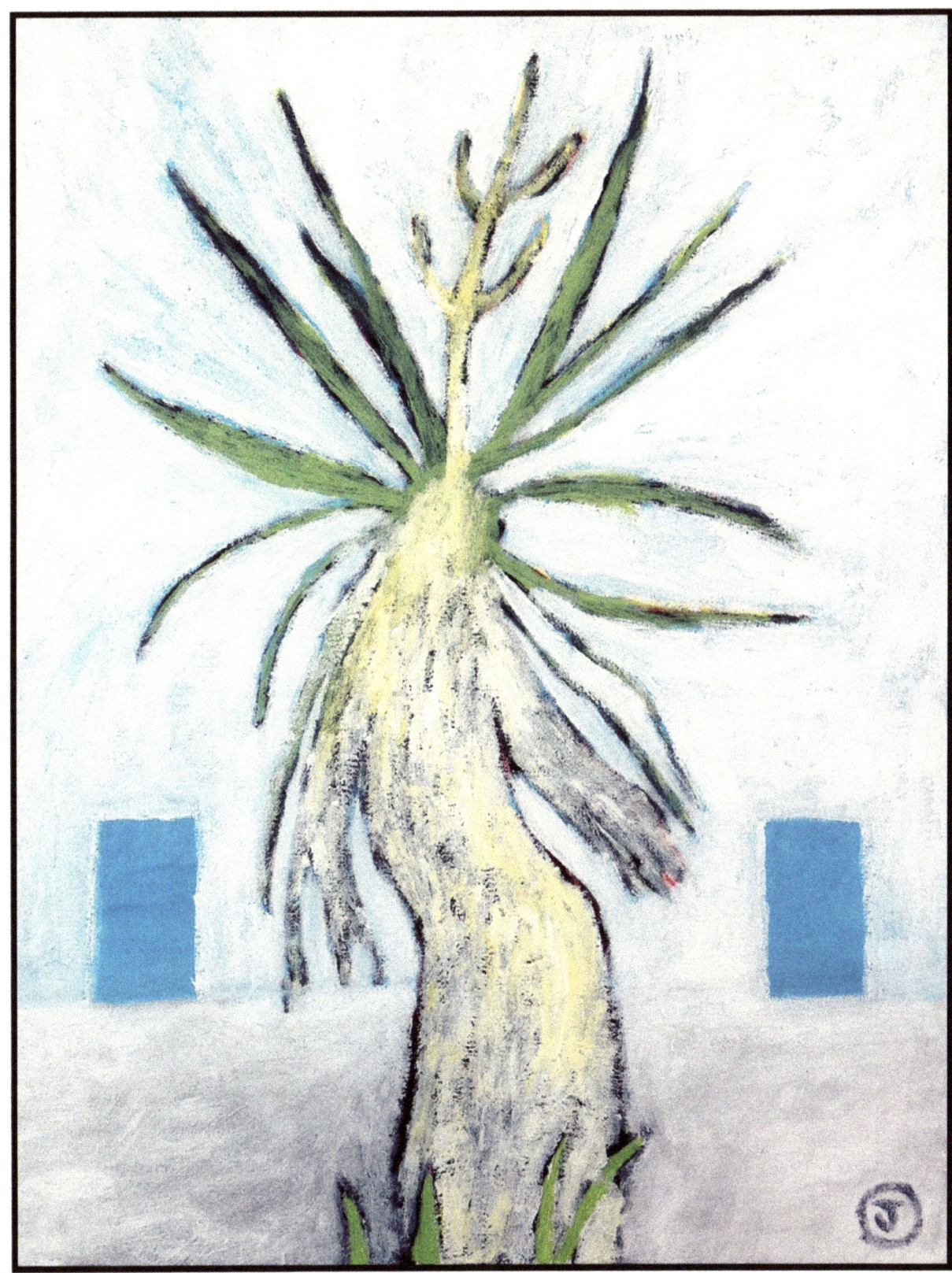

JOURNEY INTO THE SECOND SUNRISE

2016

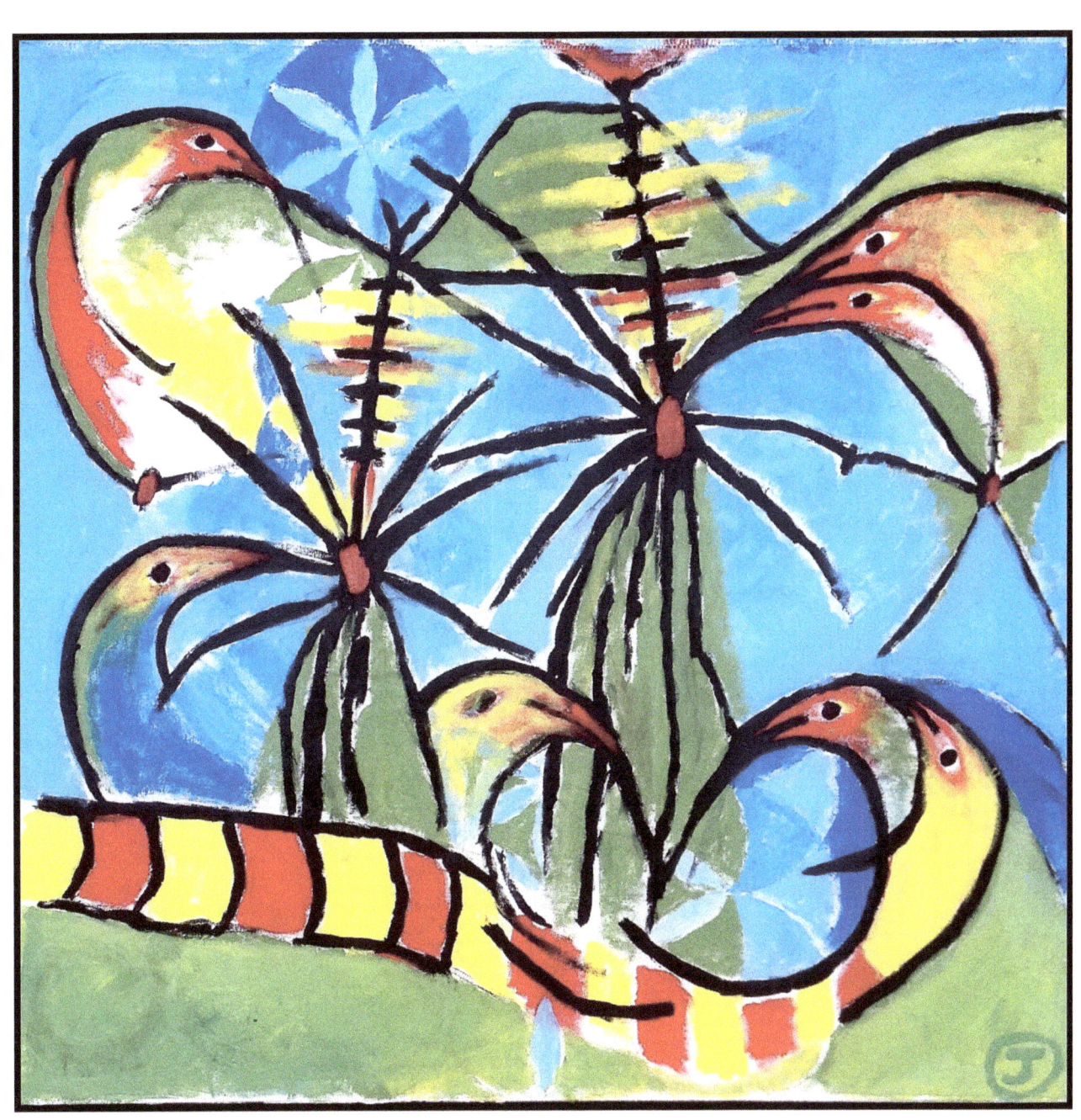

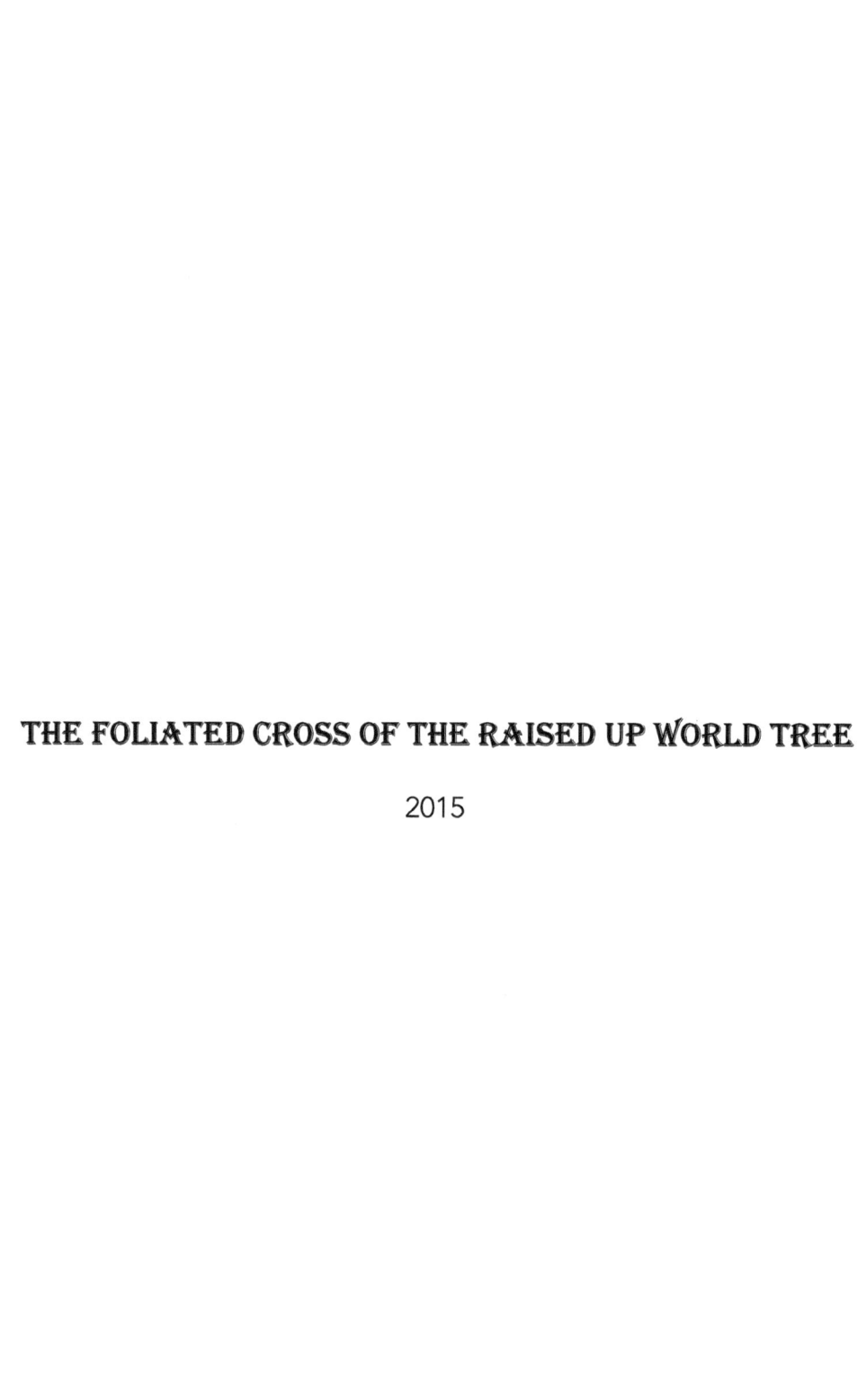

THE FOLIATED CROSS OF THE RAISED UP WORLD TREE

2015

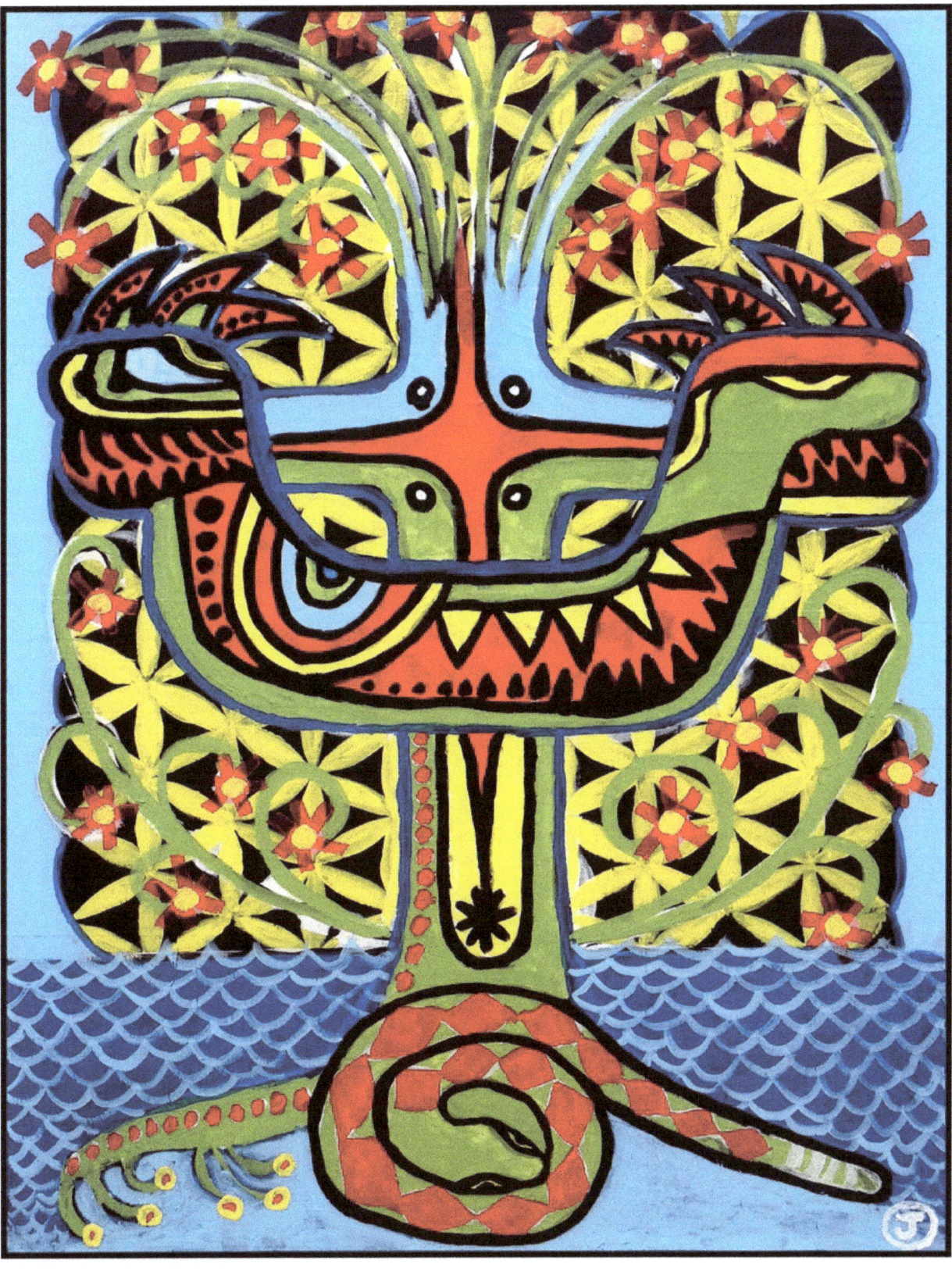

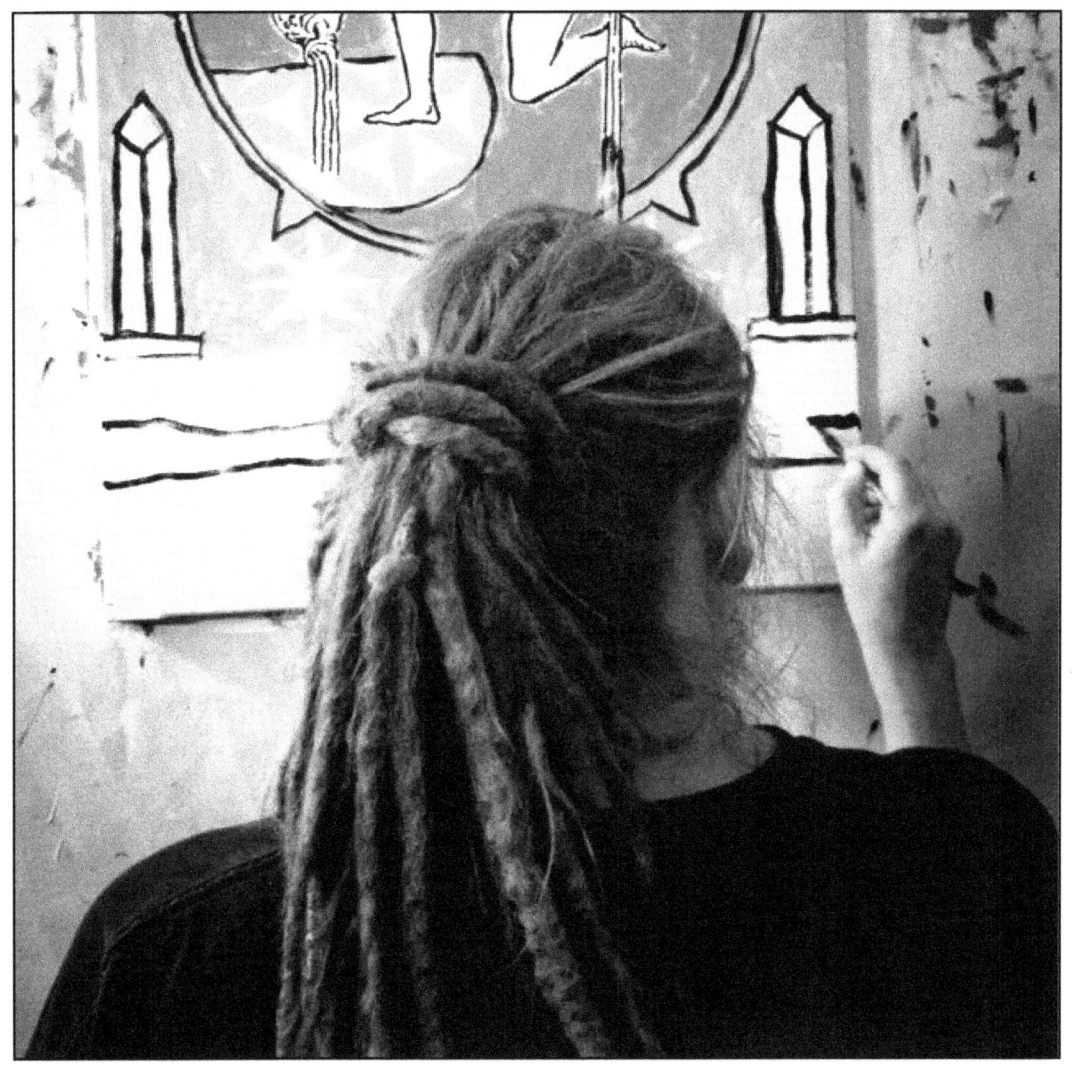

JON CHRISTOPHER was born and raised in Southern California. He lives with his love of 35 years, Tania, and their dog Suki, in the hi-desert overlooking Joshua Tree National Park. Jon is the author of four novels, including his latest, *Joe's Late Great American Dream*, which was published in 2020 on Traveling Shoes Press. He describes himself a "creatively restless" and is either writing, creating music, painting or designing books for Traveling Shoes Press. His latest project involves making videos and writing reviews of cannabis for Red Bench Reviews.

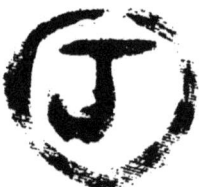

www.ingramcontent.com/pod-product-compliance
Lightning Source LLC
Chambersburg PA
CBHW040547220526
45473CB00017B/3040